The Furniture of
GUSTAV STICKLEY

History* Techniques* Projects

Joseph J. Bavaro

Thomas L. Mossman

Linden Publishing Inc.

Fresno, California

246897531

THE FURNITURE OF GUSTAV STICKLEY
History, Techniques, Projects

by

Joseph J. Bavaro

and

Thomas L. Mossman

ISBN:0-941936-35-x

Originally published by Simon & Schuster

Copyright ©1982 Van Nostrand Reinhold Company Inc.

Designed by Loudan Enterprises

Library of Congress Cataloging-in-Publication Data

Bravaro, Joseph J.
  The furniture of Gustav Stickley: history, techniques, projects/ by Joseph J. Bavaro and Thomas L. Mossman. — 1st Linden Publishing ed.

    p.   cm.
  Originally published: New York: Van Nostrand Reinhold, 1982.
  Includes bibliographical references and index.
  ISBN 0-941936-35-X
  1. Cabinetwork. 2. Furniture making — United States — History.
3. Furniture, Mission. 4. Stickley, Gustav, 1858-1942,
I. Mossman Thomas L. II. Title.
TT197.B35 1996
749.213—dc20   95-47410
                                CIP

PRINTED IN THE UNITED STATES OF AMERICA

First Linden Publishing Edition 1996

Quotations from *The Craftsman* appear on th following pages:
page 6: Volume 7, p. 53
page 6: Volume 7, p. 720
page 20: Volume 1, November 1901, Forewor
page 21: Volume 1, October 1901, Foreword
page 34: Volume 29, p. 53
pages 34–35: Volume 7, p. 54 and p. 60
page 37: Volume 4, p. 59
page 60–62: Volume 8, pp. 524–529, 533–534
pages 84–85: Volume 9, pp. 123-125
page 88: Volume 17, p. 336 and pp. 338-339
page 89: Volume 8, p. 85

Quotations from *Chips From The Craftsman Workshops* appear on the following pages:
page 17: Volume 1, pp. 2–3
page 18: Volume 1, pp. 8–9

Quotations from *Craftsman Homes* appear on the following pages:
pages 87–88: 1909, p. 162
page 88: 1909, p. 164

Linden Publishing Inc.
3845 N. Blackstone
Fresno, CA 93726
1-800-345-4447

Contents

Acknowledgments   6

Introduction   7

1. The Arts in America   8
2. Gustav Stickley—The Craftsman   17
3. A Democratic Art   33

   A Selection of Craftsman
   Furniture   39

4. Materials and Methods   60
5. Projects   89

   Mirror, 90
   Screen, 93
   Combination Bookcase and Table, 100
   Rocker, 108
   Recliner, 117
   Settle, 129
   Dining Table, 136
   Bookcase, 143
   Clock Case, 157

Bibliography   171

Index   172

Acknowledgments

We would like to express our sincere appreciation to those who were especially helpful to us in the preparation of this book. Their contributions of time, effort, and understanding are greatly appreciated, and without them, this book would not have been possible: a special thanks to Susan Lagler Mossman, whose skill and patience were invaluable, and to Mr. and Mrs. James Marrin for their generosity, support, and the loan of many Arts and Crafts items. We would also like to thank Mrs. Ben Wiles, Sr., Mrs. Louise Stickley, Mr. and Mrs. Alfred J. Audi, Eve MacCloskey (word processer), Kathy Slinkard, and Randell Makinson for their contributions to our effort.

Introduction

This book is intended as a tribute to Gustav Stickley, a pioneer in contemporary design and creator of the first truly American furniture, known throughout the world as Craftsman. A hardworking, dedicated man, Stickley achieved success in the early 1900s as the leader of the Arts and Crafts movement in America.

Were Stickley alive today, he would be immensely pleased with the increasing recognition accorded his furniture in the history of American design. But he might also be dismayed that Craftsman furniture is now so scarce and highly prized for its antique value that it exists largely in private and museum collections rather than in the homes of the working people for whom he intended it. Single pieces have commanded prices in the thousands at recent auctions; yet they were originally created for

... the real Americans ... the great middle class, possessed of moderate culture and moderate material resources. For them, art should not be allowed to remain as a subject of consideration for critics. It should be brought to their homes and become for them a part and parcel of their daily lives.

In this book, we have included an overview of developments in the arts to which Stickley fell heir, his personal story, and his philosophy to provide an understanding of the man, his accomplishments, and the times in which he lived and worked. Also included are instructions for building nine pieces of Craftsman furniture, presented with as much attention, authenticity, and detail as Stickley himself devoted to their original creation. In offering these projects, we trust that others will find, as we did, the truth of Stickley's words:

When we come to make things ourselves and because they are needed, instead of depending upon the department store to furnish them, we shall not only find more pleasure in making them, but we shall also take more pleasure in possessing them.

7

1. The Arts in America

At the Philadelphia Exhibition of 1876, the world gathered to help the United States celebrate one hundred years of independence. But those who attended the centennial festivities found independence of an industrial and political nature only, with cultural dependency apparent in the numerous poorly crafted reproductions of European taste. These ranged from copies of Greek and Roman art to Byzantine, Italian Renaissance, baroque and Louis XV reproductions. The popularity of objects based upon historical style resulted in part from an American need to identify with long-established wealth, status, and "culture."

Beaux arts furniture, with its stately, majestic style that stressed objectivity and the pursuit of formal perfection, had centuries of aristocratic and aesthetic precedence in Europe. In America, however, beaux arts pieces became objects taken out of context to satisfy a culturally dependent society. Manufacturers made little, if any, attempt to break this dependency. Inferior reproduction of furniture with which most Americans had little direct contact and, therefore, no basis of comparison, was much too profitable for them. American buyers could not know that these

1-1. Furniture display of Gardner and Company, Philadelphia Exhibition of 1876. (The Free Library of Philadelphia)

reproductions were mere shadows of the originals in terms of craftsmanship.

Two styles vied with beaux arts classicism for domination of America in the late nineteenth century: art nouveau, a European style adopted by artists seeking new forms as well as different ways to employ traditional ideas; and the Arts and Crafts movement, with British roots linked to the ideas of John Ruskin and William Morris.

Art nouveau saw nature as a source of inspiration rather than as a catalog of forms to be reproduced. Flowers and vines caught in the movement of opening and growing, insects in their immense complexity, and the tender grace and sensuousness of the female figure formed the vital and diverse base from which art nouveau flourished. The movement was adopted by a few architects and designers in America. Its popularity in the United States, though minimal and scattered, can be traced to the work of Louis C. Tiffany and Louis Sullivan, both of whom had studied in France.

The efforts of Tiffany and Sullivan and the few other art nouveau proponents in America posed no real threat to the supremacy of the beaux arts tradition. Their work, though familiar to many Americans, was limited in its popularity by its prohibitive cost and its connection to the work of European designers who used erotic imagery freely. The American public was still deeply immersed in puritanism and rarely discussed such controversial topics, let alone displayed objects in their homes with design motifs giving pictorial reality to them.

Art nouveau did receive acceptance in advertising and other

1–2. Lamp, glass-and-bronze picture frame, and glassware from Tiffany Studios, 1900–1910. (Private collection)

graphic media, however. People could enjoy these public images without taking responsibility for their existence. Posters and advertisements that employed the flowing exoticism of art nouveau abounded. In fact, the highest paid commercial artist of his day, Will H. Bradley, was often referred to as the "American Beardsley." One of Bradley's greatest contributions to American design was a unique synthesis of the decorative art nouveau and the more functional Arts and Crafts. He developed a modular type system for the creation of border designs for title

pages and advertisements. With this system, decorative borders, a hallmark of art nouveau, could be created by any skilled printer who, rather than hiring an illustrator, could assemble the modules of border type into the correct size and shape.

Bradley, an accomplished designer in the art nouveau style, became a convert to the American Arts and Crafts movement, exemplifying the relative strength of Arts and Crafts in America and its real challenge to the beaux arts tradition. In contrast to art nouveau, the Arts and Crafts movement presented reality instead of fantasy, simplicity instead of complexity, economy instead of extravagance, and distinctly native design instead of European idealism. These differences were well suited to existing middle-class values in America. The Arts and Crafts movement transformed the middle class into a desirable appellation rather than a position to escape by false identification with the upper class.

The American Arts and Crafts movement was inspired by the British movement of the same name, particularly by the writings and work of John Ruskin and William Morris. John Ruskin (1819–1900) advocated a renaissance of medieval arts. An Oxford education and an inherited fortune provided him with the freedom to travel throughout Europe promoting his ideas. The squalid working and living conditions of industrial-

ized England's working class fed the revolutionary fire of Ruskin's words. Eventually he founded the Guild of St. George, an organization of artisans who lived and worked in a cooperative effort. Printing presses and workshops in various trades were reminiscent of the medieval cottage industries idealized by Ruskin. These ventures had a widespread effect upon English taste and became an integral part of changing intellectual movements.

A disciple of Ruskin, William Morris (1834–1896) was also influenced by a group of painters known as the Pre-Raphaelite brotherhood. Beginning as a group of talented young intellectuals who found inspiration in medieval models (those created before Raphael's time), the brotherhood included such artistic geniuses as Edward Burne-Jones, John E. Millais, William Holman

1-4. John Ruskin (1819–1900). (The Free Library of Philadelphia)

1-5. William Morris (1834–1896). (*The Craftsman*, vol. VII, p. 413)

Hunt, Dante Gabriel Rossetti, and Ford Madox Brown. William Morris's goal, inherited from Ruskin, was a golden age where artists would replace industrialists and hand labor would bring workers the pleasure lacking in mass mechanical production as well as material reward for their work. In turn, the joy of labor would be evident in the item made by hand.

1-3. Interior and furniture design by Will H. Bradley, 1896, shows use of both art nouveau and Arts and Crafts styles. Designed for the *Ladies' Home Journal*.

Morris, trained in architecture, was drawn to other artistic pursuits through his friendship with Burne-Jones and Rossetti. Eventually he merged his talent and philosophy into the creation of Red House, his home outside London, where every element was designed to meet a functional necessity instead of simply a historic tradition. The house was constructed by hand, of handmade material, and furnished with Morris-designed furniture and other articles. Soon after, Morris opened a shop in London where furniture, decorative glass, pottery, textiles, paintings, and sculpture were displayed and sold. All objects shared a utilitarian and aesthetic purpose, and all were designed by Morris or his associates, Rossetti and Burne-Jones. As the popularity of the items grew, Morris's crusade for prestige for the handmade object expanded. Workshops were established for the production of wallpaper and hand-loomed fabric.

1-6. *St. George's Cabinet*, Morris and Company, 1861. Decorated by William Morris. (The Victoria and Albert Museum, London)

1-7. *Sussex Chair*, Morris and Company, 1865. (The Victoria and Albert Museum, London)

1-8. *The Backgammon Players*, Morris and Company, 1862. Decorated by Edward Burne-Jones. (The Metropolitan Museum of Art, Rogers Fund, 1926)

11

ever twixt trunk and leaf · chasing the prey · ·

Morris became increasingly socialistic in his teachings, and turned much energy to the Kelmscott Press, which produced fine, handcrafted books.

The American Arts and Crafts movement borrowed much from the English movement. Some American designers totally embraced the ideals of their British predecessors. Establishing themselves in the medieval guild philosophy, they accepted only those objects conceived and executed by the same individual, without assistance from machinery. Other designers felt this strict adherence to the philosophy of Morris and Ruskin limited the availability of their products, which could not be made at a price affordable to the average middle-class consumer. These designers rejected the implicit elitism of Morris and Ruskin and sought a solution to bring their work back into the grasp of the average working American.

The answer was the recognition of technology as an ally instead of an enemy. Designs were analyzed. Those parts that could best be made by hand were executed by hand, and those that could be made by machine without sacrificing quality of craftsmanship were executed by machine. This approach meant more pieces could be produced daily by artisans and, therefore, a larger portion of society could be served.

Simple, honest, and functional products of the Arts and Crafts movement found their way into the daily lives of many Americans by the early 1900s. Exhibitions were held to display the work of designers all over the country.

1–9. *The Woodpecker Tapestry*, William Morris, 1885. (William Morris Gallery, Walthamstow, England)

Magazines ran pictorial articles showing the work of selected craftsmen, bringing the philosophy of the movement into the homes of the people it was meant to reach.

Functional objects of everyday life—lamps, candlesticks, bookends, fireplace tools and screens, cooking utensils, pottery, textiles, windows, and furniture—were constructed of various materials. Many designers limited their production to specific household items, using only the materials to which they had apprenticed themselves in the classic medieval tradition. Also in line with this tradi-

tion, craftsmen would affix their signature to an object in the form of a mark, signifying their personal attention to its design and craftsmanship.

One such craftsman/designer was Dirk Van Erp, a Dutch coppersmith who settled in the San Francisco area in 1886. He supported himself by working in the shipyards as a metalsmith and in his leisure time, formed objects from discarded brass shell-casings. In time, these became popular among visitors to the docks and led to his opening a copper shop in Oakland, California. Because he adhered to his traditional appren-

1-12. Signature of Roycraft Enterprises, East Aurora, NY.

1-10. Magazine advertisement for R.R. Jarvie, *The House Beautiful*, 1902. Advertisements and magazine articles brought the work and philosophy of the Arts and Crafts movement to the attention of those for whom it was primarily intended: the working middle class.

1-11. Candlestick, R.R. Jarvie, c. 1904. The Jarvie shop was a well-known Chicago manufacturer of candlesticks and lanterns, examples of the typical functional objects created by Arts and Crafts designers. (Private collection)

1-13. Signature of Van Briggle Pottery Company, Colorado Springs, CO.

1-14. Signature of Dirk Van Erp, Oakland, CA.

ticeship training, Van Erp maintained that every object produced by his shop should be made solely by hand. Although he had a very limited formal design education, he was gifted with a natural sensitivity for metal and created forms perfectly suited to that material. Lamps, bowls, vases, plates, bookends, desk sets, and other hand-wrought pieces were the products of his professional activity, which spanned approximately twenty years.

Elbert Hubbard was another individual who achieved tremendous success in the Arts and Crafts era, largely by virtue of his flamboyant nature and talent in salesmanship. In fact, his fame was such that his name continues to be synonymous with American Arts and Crafts.

Having made his fortune as a soap salesman, Hubbard became enamoured of socialism and the revival of the guilds. In 1893 he visited William Morris's Kelmscott Press in England and returned home to establish a guild known as the Roycrofters, which engaged in the art of bookmaking. Stock in the corporation was owned by the workers, making this a true cooperative. The culmination of Hubbard's efforts several years later included the construction of a medieval manor in East Aurora, New York, complete with a workers' community. Roycroft workshops were a great success, producing a variety of Arts and Crafts items, including books, metalwork, decorative items, and a line of Roycroft furniture. Although Hubbard and his wife died with the sinking of the *Lusitania* in 1915, the Roycroft establishment continued successfully for a number of years thereafter.

Many potteries and tile companies were in operation during this period, producing what was called art pottery. Rookwood Pottery of Cincinnati, Ohio; Grueby Faience and Tile Company of Boston, Massachusetts; Fulper Pottery Company of Flemington, New Jersey; Paul Revere Pottery of Boston, Massachusetts; S. A. Weller of Zanesville, Ohio; Marblehead Pottery of Marblehead,

1-15. Copper lamps with mica shades, Dirk Van Erp, c. 1915. (Private collection)

1-16. Copper bowl, book cover, and candlestick, Dirk Van Erp, c. 1913. (Private collection)

Massachusetts; and Van Briggle Pottery Company of Colorado Springs, Colorado; were some of the most notable examples. For the most part, these companies were started by craftspeople with an interest in ceramics and glazes in the French and oriental tradition. They filtered these interests through the British craft guild philosophy of William Morris and added highlights of their native American culture. The synthesis of these influences gave American art pottery its characteristic and unique aesthetic elements— simple, incised, hand-decorated images of plant and animal forms emerging from the body of the object, which was usually one color (though sometimes detailed in contrasting colors) covered with a heavy layer of matte glaze that softened the contours of the carved or built-up surface.

All the objects produced during the Arts and Crafts movement were designed for the enhancement of man's environment. This living space, whether home or office, was conceived and executed with the same concerns of honesty to material, simplicity of form, and practicality of function characteristic of pottery, furniture, and metalcraft of the period. In architecture, this philosophy was most successfully applied by Charles and Henry Greene, two brothers whose work epitomizes Arts and Crafts ideals at their highest level.

The mature Greene and Greene style developed gradually through periods influenced by exposure to the interiors of William Morris, adaptations of the Swiss mountain chalet, and the motifs and structure of Japanese architecture. Their love of oriental architecture, with its emphasis on horizontal lines and simple floor plans, com-

bined with the local Californian, shingled bungalow style, produced a series of homes that reflected the Arts and Crafts philosophy carried to its most uncompromised state.

The Greenes believed in creating a totally designed environment. They determined the needs of their client and then formulated a design concept that encom-

1-17. Hammered copper bookends, Roycroft, c. 1910. (Private collection)

1-18. Art pottery. Left to right: Rookwood, Marblehead, Paul Revere, Fulper, and Grueby; 1902–1915. (Private collection)

1-19. Robert R. Blacker house, designed by Charles and Henry Greene, 1907–1909.

passed the home, site, and furnishings. The structure of the house, its joints and motifs, were repeated in appropriate scale in each piece of furniture, rug, light fixture, and accessory for the house. Craftsmen were hired to work in various media under the close scrutiny of the Greenes, each contributing to the project their special skills and reflecting the Greenes' uncompromising philosophy.

Furniture design was an important part of the Arts and Crafts revolution in America, and its true leader was Gustav Stickley, creator of the Craftsman style. Simply designed, functional, "democratic" pieces in native woods (especially oak), remarkable for their excellent craftsmanship and natural finish, were painstakingly designed by Stickley. In his magazine, *The Craftsman*, begun in 1901, Stickley expounded his personal philosophy and brought to the public his revolutionary furniture designs as well as the work of his contemporaries in what he termed the "Craftsman Movement."

By 1904, the Arts and Crafts movement had spread across most of America. Its popularity can be attributed to many factors, foremost among them the public exposure provided by its self-appointed leader and spokesman, Gustav Stickley.

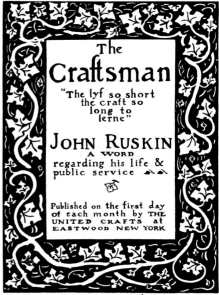

VOL.I   November, MDCCCCI   NO.2

The Craftsman

"The lyf so short the craft so long to lerne"

JOHN RUSKIN
A WORD regarding his life & public service

Published on the first day of each month by THE UNITED CRAFTS at EASTWOOD NEW YORK

Price 20 cents the copy

1-20. Cover of *The Craftsman*, November, 1901. This issue was devoted to John Ruskin. (Private collection)

2. Gustav Stickley—The Craftsman

In the small town of Osceola, Wisconsin, on March 9, 1857, a son was born to Leopold and Barbara Stoeckel; Gustav (originally spelled with a final *e*) was the first of eleven children. Leopold Stickley (the family name was later Americanized) was a farmer and stonemason, providing for his large family by hard labor in the fields and the building trade. His eldest son had to start working at age twelve to help support the family. Apprenticed as a stonemason, Gustav recalled that he

had worked as a stone mason from the stage of mixing and carrying mortar up to that of cutting and laying the stone. It was heavy and tedious labor, much too hard for a boy of my age, and being put to it so early gave me an intense dislike for it. . . . I have always felt that it is to this I owe my immediate and lasting delight in working in the comparatively soft and yielding wood, and my quick appreciation of its qualities—an appreciation that has made possible all that I have been able to do.

Within a few years, Gustav's father abandoned the family, and Gustav took on the responsibility of looking after his mother and ten young brothers and sisters. Leaving school in the eighth grade was a bitter disappointment to him, but he worked hard, cutting and hauling wood to market, looking after the farm, and working as a mason. His early experience working with his hands, making farm implements and household

items for the family, laid the foundation for his lifelong dedication to the recognition of handcrafts as noble and worthy pursuits.

When Gustav was sixteen, his mother accepted the offer of her brother, Schuyler C. Brandt, to join him in Pennsylvania. The family moved in 1874 to the town of Brandt, where Schuyler owned a furniture factory. Gustav was employed by his uncle and accompanied him on peddling jaunts around the countryside, selling brooms and ironing boards. He also worked in the factory, where plain wooden and cane-seated chairs were manufactured.

To work with wood in this modest plant was undoubtedly a great relief to a boy who had spent so much of his childhood in heavy labor under the shadow of tremendous responsibility. He described these years with his uncle as the time from which "I can date my love for working in wood and my appreciation of the beauty and interest to be found in its natural color, texture, and grain . . . ."

Stickley also resumed his education by reading in his uncle's library. The works of John Ruskin and Thomas Carlyle were well represented, and he became especially interested in Ruskin, and later, logically, in William Morris.

By the age of twenty-one, Stickley was manager and foreman of

2-1. Gustav Stickley, the Craftsman (1857-1942).

the Brandt Chair Company. He was experienced in woodworking, steeped in Ruskin's philosophy, and full of youth and vigor; he was ready to combine these influences into independent action. On September 12, 1883, Gustav married Eda Simmons of Susquehanna, and the next year he and two younger brothers, Charles and Albert, opened a wholesale and retail furniture business in Binghamton, New York. Stickley Brothers sold Brandt chairs and period reproduction furniture made in Grand Rapids, the furniture-manufacturing capital in Michigan.

Business was poor at first, and though the brothers employed a uniquely humorous advertising campaign, they were struggling.

An offer of financial support came if Stickley Brothers would manufacture in Binghamton and, according to Stickley:

. . . the story of how we did this is really the story of how I came to undertake handmade furniture. Before any capital would be put into the concern, it was necessary to show that we were actually manufacturing, and we had no money to buy machinery. I went to a maker of broomhandles who had a good turning-lathe which he used only a part of the time. I hired the use of this, and with it blocked out the plainer parts of some very simple chairs made after the "Shaker" model. The rest of them I made by hand, with the aid of a few simple and inexpensive machines which were placed in the loft of the store. . . . The wood in shape was dried in the sun on the tin roof of the building. The very primitiveness of this equipment, made necessary by lack of means, furnished what was really a golden opportunity to break away from the monotony of commercial forms, and I turned my attention to reproducing by hand some of the simplest and best models of the old Colonial, Windsor and other plain chairs and to a study of this period as a foundation for original work along the same lines.

Stickley had visited Shaker communities, and Shaker furniture was known in the area since it had been exhibited at the Philadelphia Exhibition of 1876. These simple chairs produced by Stickley Brothers were a refreshing change from the heavy, overly ornamented parlor suites of the preceding decade, and soon became quite popular. Other manufacturers began to produce similar products but with a greater use of machinery and little attention to detail, an aspect which Stickley felt so important to the integrity of the pieces. Imitators added novelties and ornamentation to make their chairs distinctive, but these were so poorly done and so out of keeping with the original simplicity of the designs that Stickley was disgusted

2-2. Mrs. Eda Simmons Stickley (18??–1919)

with the results of the trend he had started. This experience was to repeat itself throughout Stickley's career.

In 1888 Stickley left Stickley Brothers, though it continued as a sales operation in Binghamton

under his brothers, Charles, Albert, and George, who had joined the firm. Always independent in nature, Gustav struck out in several directions. He became the vice-president of the Binghamton Street Railway, a pioneer in electrically equipped trolley transportation. He also supervised the workshops of the Auburn Prison, and he and his family moved to Auburn. But the furniture business was thoroughly ingrained in the man, and while working at Auburn, he began setting up a business in Syracuse to sell and manufacture furniture.

In 1893, leaving his family in Auburn, he took a room at the new Yates Hotel in Syracuse to finish plans for the new business, to be located on Clinton Street. He and his partner called themselves the Stickley-Simonds Company. This brief stay at the Yates marked the introduction of one of the most influential friends in Stickley's life, for Dr. Irene Sar-

2-3. Shaker furniture grouping (The Shaker Museum, Old Chatham, New York; Photo by Louis H. Frohman)

18

gent also roomed at the hotel. A professor of Romance languages at Syracuse University and a critic of art and architecture, Dr. Sargent taught Stickley French and helped to further his interest in European artistic developments, which were to have a great influence upon him.

Within the year Stickley moved his family to Syracuse. Work was progressing on the downtown shop and on the workshops, which occupied twenty-eight acres of land in nearby Eastwood, a suburb of Syracuse. Two brothers, Leopold and J. George, came to work with Gustav at Stickley-Simonds; after a few years, they quit and started their own company in Fayetteville, outside of Syracuse.

The first furniture produced by Stickley-Simonds was reproduction Windsor, Chippendale, and other simple chairs, much as Stickley had manufactured in Binghamton. In 1898 Simonds left the partnership and Stickley visited Europe. With his newly learned French, childhood German, and background from reading and discussions of trends in European arts with Dr. Sargent, he planned to witness firsthand the art nouveau and Arts and Crafts styles. In France he met Samuel Bing, Lalique, and other leaders of the art nouveau movement at Bing's Maison l'art nouveau and purchased samples of metalwork, glass, ceramics, textiles, and furniture. He also visited the masters of the Arts and Crafts movement in England—Ashbee, Voysee, and Lethaby—and collected examples of Arts and Crafts work as well.

Upon his return to the United States, Stickley changed the name of his company to the Gustav Stickley Company and began de-

2–4. Stickley furniture display at Pan-American Exposition of 1901 in Buffalo, NY. (Buffalo and Erie County Historical Society)

signing a new line of furniture. He tried some art nouveau pieces but was never happy with the results, and they were commercially produced only on a limited basis. The Arts and Crafts style was more in keeping with Stickley's love of simplicity and his desire to provide furniture appropriate to the common man's way of life and economic reach.

A very basic, almost primitive, style emerged from Stickley's hand, which he called "structural." It was extremely simple, with a medieval flavor, and featured little ornamentation except for the structural elements of the construction—the joints and dowels that held the piece together.

Structural furniture was exhibited at the Grand Rapids Furniture Market in 1900, and though it did not receive raves from the retailers, the noted magazine *The House Beautiful* praised Stickley's line, calling it "sensible furniture." In 1901 Stickley showed room set-

tings at the Pan-American Exposition in Buffalo, New York, in a joint exhibit with the Grueby Faience Company of Boston.

The Grueby Faience Company was founded by William H. Grueby in 1894. Grueby was one of the first manufacturers of ceramics to use matte glaze. At first his work was based on historical models, but by 1899 the Grueby form was established and continued throughout the firm's existence.

His pottery was characterized by dense matte glazes, generally dark green, but sometimes yellow, brown, blue, or red. The body surfaces were often decorated with plant forms in low relief. Tiles manufactured by Grueby also used botanical forms, and some featured scenic decoration.

Grueby pottery and tiles were a perfect complement to Stickley's furniture. Stickley was quite fond of Grueby's work, and Craftsman furniture and Grueby tiles and pottery were seen together in many places. Grueby pieces sitting on Craftsman tables and bookcases and Grueby tile fireplaces were frequently illustrated in *The Craftsman* magazine. Stickley even inlaid the tops of several models of small tables with Grueby tiles. (Though Grueby's work met with popular acclaim, the firm struggled financially and finally declared bankruptcy in 1908.)

The Syracuse business took several years to become established. Stickley continually refined his thinking and applied his philosophy to the design of the furniture he planned to produce and to the organization of the workshops. He called the production shop The United Crafts, reflecting the medieval influences of the guild system so enthusiastically espoused by Ruskin and Morris.

2-5. Advertisement for Grueby pottery, which frequently appeared with Stickley's furniture. *The Craftsman*

GRUEBY POTTERY

GOLD MEDAL PARIS 1900

GRUEBY FAIENCE CO., BOSTON MASS

2-6. Early signature, c. 1901, with Stickley's initials, G. S., in the center of the compass.

2-7. Signature variations from 1902-1912.

Stickley set up a profit-sharing plan and considered himself more master craftsman than employer. Furthermore, Stickley felt that all the furniture he designed should be built under one roof so that the quality, color, and feel of the pieces would be harmonious. In keeping with the guild theory, a mark was chosen to act as the official signature of the organization. Stickley chose the motto *Als ik kan*, "if I can," which he adopted from William Morris. As Stickley later described it, the mark represented many things:

In the Middle Ages, that golden period of the arts and crafts, each master-workman adopted some device or legend which, displayed upon every object of his creation, came finally to represent his individuality as completely as did his face, or his voice; making him known beyond the burgher circle in which he passed his life. . . . Among the legends so employed, the one assumed by Ian van Eyck, the early Flemish painter, has retained its force and point down to our own day. "Als ich kanne" (if I can) appears written across the canvases of this fourteenth century chef d'ecole, placed there, without doubt, as an inspiration toward excellence in that art wherein van Eyck became an epoch maker. . . .

. . . when William Morris, in his early manhood, visited the Low Countries, and there grew fired with enthusiasm for the decorative arts, he found this legend and made it his own. He used it, in French translation . . . Si je puis. . . .

This legend in its modern Flemish form, Als ik kan, has been adopted by the Master of the United Crafts. It here forms an interesting device with a joiner's compass, which is the most primitive and distinctive tool of the worker in wood. The legend is further accompanied by the signature of the Master of the Crafts, Gustav Stickley, which, together with the proper date, appears branded upon every object produced in the workshop of the Guild.

The rapid changes in the early years of Stickley's career can be traced by the changes in his mark.

Several different versions were used until 1912, when a mark was established that remained the Stickley symbol.

Stickley also founded *The Craftsman* magazine in 1901, which sold for twenty cents a copy. The foreword of the first issue of the magazine outlined the ideals and goals of the United Crafts:

The United Crafts endeavor to promote and to extend the principles established by Morris, in both the artistic and the socialistic sense. In the interests of art, they seek to substitute the luxury of taste for the luxury of costliness; to teach that beauty does not imply elaboration or ornament; to employ only those forms and materials which make for simplicity, individuality and dignity of effect.

. . . "It is right and necessary that all men should have work to do which shall be worth doing, and be pleasant to do; and which should be done under such conditions as would make it neither over-wearisome, nor over-anxious" [William Morris].

With this example before them, The United Crafts will labor to produce in their workshops only those articles which shall justify their own creation; which shall serve some actual and important end in the household. . . . Thus, it is hoped to co-operate with those many and earnest minds who are seeking to create a national, or rather a universal art, adjusted to the needs of the century: an art developed by the people, as a reciprocal joy for the artist and the layman.

The magazine's first issues were dedicated to Ruskin and Morris and followed Morris's Kelmscott Press tradition with a small format, rough paper, and woodcut vignettes. Irene Sargent wrote five articles on William Morris for the first issue and continued to be a major contributor to the magazine for many years. Stickley himself

VOL. 1   October, MDCCCCI   NO. 1

2-8. Cover design of the first issue of *The Craftsman*

2-9. Joiners at work, Eastwood factory. (*The Craftsman*)

2-10. Rush-seat workers, Eastwood factory. (*The Craftsman*)

2-11. Interior of the Butterick Publishing Company, New York, 1904, contains early Stickley office furniture and windows by Louis C. Tiffany and Company. (Museum of the City of New York)

The first Craftsman Building included a bindery, library, furniture showrooms, drafting, design and editorial offices, and a public lecture hall. It opened its doors to the public on December 1, 1902, with a lecture in French by a member of the prestigious Alliance Française, the first of many public lectures and events to be held in United Crafts Hall. Later speakers included Frank Lloyd Wright, Louis Sullivan, and Louis C. Tiffany. It became quite a popular meeting place, and Stickley enjoyed using it as a gathering spot for those in sympathy with his ideas.

1902 was a landmark year in another respect: house designs first appeared in *The Craftsman* indicating Stickley's increasing interest in the total environment as an extension of his furniture designs. Dr. Sargent continued to be a mainstay of the magazine, but Stickley was taking an increasing interest in expressing his own thoughts and those of his contemporaries in the arts, both at home and abroad.

wrote on the evolution of his structural style and the relation between its form and his views on the value of simplicity in life and his love for wood.

The first Stickley furniture, like the first issues of *The Craftsman*, demonstrated Stickley's immersion in the medieval. The furniture was massive, and the hardware was chemically treated to give it the appearance of age. Still, the basic elements of his style were present, and as they were refined, a new purity of form from function emerged.

By 1902 Stickley needed a larger headquarters. The magazine was doing well, and the furniture business was growing. Stickley purchased an unusual four-story stone building, the Crouse Stables, and remodeled it to accommodate his growing concerns. The building was designed by Archimedes Russel for Edgar Crouse, son of the Crouse College benefactor. Angry that his father had spent so much

money on a girl's school, the son commissioned a stable for his horses by the same architect and spent an incredible amount of money to make it as lavish as his father's donation to the school. (The original Crouse Hall still stands on the Syracuse University campus.)

2-12. The first Craftsman Building, Syracuse; formerly the Crouse Stables. (*The Craftsman*)

The magazine soon took on a new format, larger in size and scope. By its second year, it ran over a hundred pages per issue and included articles on social reform and industrial education, architecture, ceramics, and Japanese art. (Stickley was a collector of Japanese prints, and many Arts and Crafts devotees were influenced by the Orient.)

In March, 1903, the Arts and Crafts Exhibition opened in the United Crafts Hall and included the work of more than one hundred American craftsmen and groups. American Indian crafts were represented, as were examples of European Arts and Crafts workmanship and even some art nouveau pieces from Bing's shop in Paris. Stickley had traveled to Europe early that year to collect items for the show and others to market in the United States under the Craftsman label. The exhibition was a success and "commanded respectful attention from the seaboard cities, and drew many professional visitors from distant Universities."

By this time, Stickley's success was clearly evident. His Craftsman furniture was prospering, and his magazine had become the voice of the Arts and Crafts movement. A variety of textiles, lamps, linens, and other furnishings had been added to the Craftsman line. Stickley turned more energy to convincing people of the merits of Craftsman furniture through his

writings and people listened. A significant article appeared in *The House Beautiful:* "The Structural Style in Cabinet-Making" defined Stickley's furniture and his aesthetic eloquently and clearly.

In 1903 Stickley was first identified as an architect in the Syracuse city directory, and the Craftsman building added a textile division. These developments indicated Stickley's growing interest in the total environment. House plans continued to appear in *The Craftsman*, and Harvey Ellis's illustrations brought to them a special quality. Ellis shared Stickley's love of natural materials, and Oriental influences can be seen in his work.

2-15. Hammered copper articles produced by the United Crafts.

Ellis had been designing everything from homes to textiles for some years by the time he became associated with Stickley. Many of his designs were used in Stickley textiles. He also created some unusually beautiful and sensitive inlaid furniture for the Craftsman line. He was a rather tragic romantic figure and worked for Stickley only six months before his death. Stickley eulogized him in *The Craftsman* as "a man of unusual gifts; possessing an accurate and exquisite sense of color, a great facility in design and a sound

2-13. Lecture hall, the Craftsman Building, Syracuse. Many notable speakers lectured in this popular meeting place. (*The Craftsman*)

2-14. A Craftsman interior. (*The Craftsman*)

23

judgment of effect. . . . Altogether, he is to be regretted as one who possessed the sacred fire of genius."

Stickley was forty-seven in 1904, the father of five girls and a boy. A strict disciplinarian, Stick-ley apparently ruled his household in accordance with his German background and belief in the work ethic. The family did not accompany Stickley on his trips abroad: Mrs. Stickley minded the children, never leaving them to the care of strangers, while her husband searched out his contemporaries, exchanged ideas, and purchased goods.

In 1904 Stickley began the Craftsman Homebuilders' Club in *The Craftsman*. In this column he offered advice to homebuilders on materials and techniques, and even included complete house plans in each issue. In Stickley's words:

I saw that the way a man's house was planned and built had as much influence upon his family's health and happiness as had the furniture they lived with. Besides, such unassuming furnishings as mine were out of place in elaborate over-ornamented interiors. They needed the sort of rooms and woodwork and exterior that would be in keeping with their own more homelike qualities. They suggested, by their sturdy build and friendly finish, an equally sturdy and friendly type of architecture. This being the case, why not build the kind of homes that would be in sympathy with the Craftsman ideal? Thus was evolved what has since come to be known as Craftsman architecture.

Craftsman houses contained open, large rooms with simple floor plans, exposed beams, a generous use of wood and a fireplace in a comfortable living room to encourage family togetherness. Bungalow-style and shingle-style houses were among the first to be featured in *The Craftsman* and the houses Stickley designed followed this pattern.

In the following year, 1905, Stickley felt it was time to move to the center of activity in the East. The offices of *The Craftsman* as well as the design and drafting departments were moved from Syracuse to New York City.

With the move to New York, Irene Sargent's long and influential association with the publication came to an end. But by this time, the magazine was attracting many contributors, including

DINING-ROOM FROM A CRAFTSMAN HOUSE—*The Craftsman, July, 1903.*

The Craftsman Homebuilders' Club

Every Member Receives FREE

COMPLETE PLANS AND SPECIFICATIONS FOR A CRAFTSMAN HOUSE

THE CRAFTSMAN is a magazine devoted to the New Domestic Art. Each issue for the year 1904 will present a design for a house in the simple, structural style in which every architectural detail serves a well-defined constructive use. These houses are provided with Furniture in which the same purpose is strictly followed ; the decorative features largely resulting from the introduction of proper color in woods, leather, and textiles. These designs include a wide range of dwellings: City and Country Houses, Farm Houses, Seashore Cottages, and Forest Lodges; the building costs ranging between $2,000 and $15,000. Two numbers of The Craftsman, November, 1903, describing the organization of the Homebuilders' Club, and January, 1904, containing the design of the first Homebuilder's House, will be mailed to any address upon the receipt of 25 cents. Also, any further information will be supplied upon request made to

GUSTAV STICKLEY

No. 14 THE CRAFTSMAN BUILDING   -   SYRACUSE, N. Y.

2-16. Advertisement for the Craftsman Homebuilders' Club. (*The Craftsman*)

2–17. A Craftsman interior. (*The Craftsman*)

noted architects Irving Gill, Charles and Henry Greene, and Grosvenor Atterbury.

The March, 1905, issue of *The Craftsman* carried another new feature, "Home Training in Cabinet-Work," which encouraged readers to build their own furniture. Stickley shared many specific details of construction and finishing from methods used in his workshops. (Some of these projects appear later in this book.) By 1905 United Crafts had become the Craftsman Workshops.

As is the case with most successful trends, many followed in the path so laboriously cut by Stickley and other leaders in modern furniture design. Many imitators sprang up in the early 1900s, manufacturing what had been dubbed "mission furniture." The term *mission* was a misnomer from the first, invented by a salesman who thought the primitive quality of furniture reminiscent of Californian missions. The name stuck, and Craftsman furniture and imitations of it have been known collectively as mission style ever since.

Among Stickley's competitors were his brothers. Trained largely in his employ, they all went into business independently and reaped success in imitating Gustav's line. Many other manufacturers also produced furniture similar to Stickley's and marketed it under

2–18. Furniture catalog, L. and J. G. Stickley. (Private collection)

25

names reminiscent of Craftsman: Mission, Hand-Craft, Arts and Crafts, Crafts-Style, Quaint, Cloister Style Life-Time Furniture, and Limbert's Holland Dutch Arts and Crafts were among the prominent names. In Stickley's view, the problem was not that he should have inspired others to like accomplishments, but that his competitors generally produced inferior-quality products and then confused the public by marketing them under names so similar to Craftsman.

That Stickley was being im-

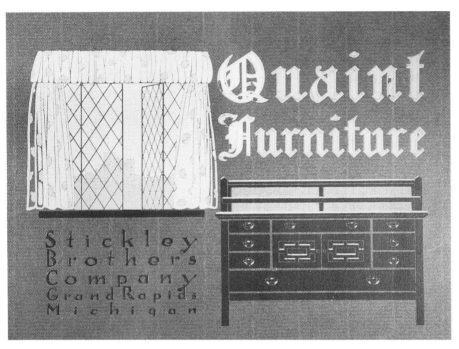

2-19. Quaint furniture catalog, Stickley Brothers, 1914. (Private collection)

2-20. Charles P. Limbert advertisement, *The Craftsman*, 1910.

itated indicates, however, just how successful he had become in only a few years. Stickley's name appeared in *Who's Who* in 1906; among his affiliations were the New York Athletic Club, the Engineer's Club, the National Arts Club, and the Society of Craftsmen. Obviously, the leader of the Arts and Crafts movement was well ensconced in a variety of social as well as professional activities, but Stickley's heart must have been turning elsewhere.

Six hundred acres in Morris Plains, New Jersey, became the site of the next Stickley enterprise—Craftsman Farms. In 1908, partly because of his love of natural environments and manual training, perhaps in reaction to city life and the increasing urbanization of the nation in general, Stickley decided to return to the land. He planned to build the most American of homes—a log cabin. But this log house was to be more than a country cottage; it was Stickley's plan that it be a clubhouse and meeting place for his friends and followers. The main house was built along these lines, and the Stickley family lived there. A number of homes were planned for the site; some guest cottages were built, but the family continued to live in the main house. The farm took shape with the planting of crops and raising of livestock. Stickley had returned to the farm, though certainly in a style much different from that of his boyhood.

Around this time a new publication, to be called *The Yeoman*, was considered, but it never reached publication. Instead, *The Craftsman* took on a less aesthetic and cosmopolitan tone and became more practical, with an increasing number of articles de-

2-21. The main house at Craftsman Farms. (*The Craftsman*)

2-22. Guest cottages at Craftsman Farms. (*The Craftsman*)

2-23. Dining room, Craftsman Farms. (*The Craftsman*)

2-24. Living room, Craftsman Farms. (*The Craftsman*)

2-25. Fireplace detail, Craftsman Farms. The inscription hammered into the copper fireplace hood reads, "The lyf so short, the craft so long to lerne." (*The Craftsman*)

voted to gardening and home care. Stickley's Homebuilders' Club had grown, and his furniture was being sold throughout the country from more than fifty franchised outlets. Craftsman houses were built in almost every community, and three years later the Craftsman Contracting Company was organized to build Stickley-designed homes. Stickley's holdings were obviously vast: he even owned sawmills in the Adirondacks, where the wood for Craftsman furniture was milled.

Having expressed himself for some years on the subject of education, Stickley put his theories into practice by opening a school for boys at Craftsman Farms.

Here he offered "a practical education," believing that farm work would teach the values so difficult to instill in strictly academic programs. The joy of working with one's hands and the satisfactions to be found in the manual arts were favorite subjects in *The Craftsman*; Stickley also suggested that such training could provide a needed sense of worth and accomplishment in the rehabilitation of criminals.

Meanwhile, in New York, Stickley was at work on the crowning touch of his multitude of ventures. Having united all his enterprises under the name of The Craftsman, Inc., he combined them all, except for the farm and workshops,

2-26. Craftsman furniture advertisement appearing above a Grueby pottery advertisement. (*House Beautiful*)

under one roof. On October 20, 1913, the new Craftsman Building opened to the public. The twelve-story structure at 6 East Thirty-ninth Street was the culmination of all of Stickley's efforts—an incarnation of the Craftsman ideal.

The four lower floors were devoted to showrooms for Craftsman furniture, rugs, draperies, textiles, and accessories. The top floors housed editorial and business offices, Craftsman clubrooms, a lecture hall, and library. The middle floors were known as the Permanent Home Builders' Exposition. Every manner of product, from wood to paint and plaster, roofing and plumbing materials,

flooring, tools, and hardware, was displayed. Indoor gardens and grassy lawns with plantings and working fountains were found in the fifth floor's "Gardens and Grounds" department. The top of the building housed the Craftsman Restaurant, which offered a varied menu of delicious dishes to guests comfortably seated on Craftsman

2-28. First floor showroom for furniture and fittings in the new Craftsman Building. (*The Craftsman*)

2-27. The new Craftsman Building, 6 East 39th Street, New York. (*The Craftsman*)

2-29. Craftsman room display on the first floor of the new Craftsman Building. (*The Craftsman*)

2–30. The Craftsman Restaurant on the top floor of the new Craftsman Building. (*The Craftsman*)

furniture. All foods served at the restaurant were grown at Craftsman Farms.

Stickley enjoyed his prominence from his lofty offices atop The Craftsman Building. He had come a long way from his humble beginnings, and yet he had never really left them behind. For all his success, his sincere motives had been to improve the lot of the common man, to educate him, to make his life more pleasant, more comfortable, and more beautiful.

On March 24, 1915, two years after the opening of the Craftsman Building, Gustav Stickley was declared bankrupt. The great entrepreneurial effort of the building and the incorporation of all the Craftsman enterprises had contributed to this fate; moreover, the Arts and Crafts movement had

peaked and waned; Colonial Revival was on the rise.

Typically, Stickley was in the process of developing a line of furniture called Chromewald, which had a new finish whereby color was impregnated in the wood. Shown at the Grand Rapids furniture exhibition of 1916, it did not meet with favorable response. He also designed some Chinese Chippendale furniture, but it was never produced for market on a large scale. By the end of 1916, Stickley's holdings were slipping quickly away.

The last issue of *The Craftsman* appeared in December, 1916. Hired as a consultant by the Simmonds Mattress Company of Kenosha, Wisconsin, Stickley returned to his native state, but the arrangement proved shortlived. In

1918 Craftsman Farms was sold to the Farney family (of the Wurlitzer Company), and Gustav's brother Leopold, of L. & J. G. Stickley, Fayetteville, bought the Eastwood factory where Craftsman furniture had been born. The May 16, 1918, issue of *Furniture World* magazine carried a notice for a new Stickley company, listing Leopold as president, Gustav as vice-president, and J. George as treasurer. A year later, however, Gustav's name was no longer associated with this enterprise. Craftsman-like furniture was produced at Eastwood until 1927, when the Colonial reproduction Cherry Valley line began.

The following year, Stickley's wife, Eda, had a fatal stroke, and he moved to the home of his daughter Barbara. Though he

2-31. Gustav with grandaughter Barbara, c. 1916.

furniture. It has stood the test of time, and many fine examples remain. Attesting to the fact that excellent craftsmanship, carefully chosen oak, and patient finishing would produce a thing of enduring beauty, a Craftsman table, chair, desk, or bookcase remains a classic—a complement to any surrounding as honest as it is—a strong, solid, whole, beautifully simple example of the Craftsman ideal.

2-32. Gustav in later years.

never again worked as he had in the Craftsman years, Stickley was never idle. He tutored Barbara's children and continued to design. He planned the Village Waterworks in Skaneateles, New York, and built a log cabin for his daughter's family on Lake Skaneateles. And for the next twenty-five years he continually worked with wood finishes, one of the interests that led to the creation of his Craftsman furniture. His daughter recalled, "We would sometimes come home and find my father with several drawers pulled out, testing a new penetrating finish formula on the bottoms."

Gustav Stickley died on April 20, 1942, at the age of eighty-five. The workmen from Eastwood took the day off to attend his funeral. Though they had been denied permission to do so, they came to say good-by to the Master Craftsman.

The most lasting and fitting tribute to Gustav Stickley is his

3. A Democratic Art

Gustav Stickley's deep-rooted nationalistic fervor was a key factor in the formulation of his aesthetic philosophy. Stickley reasoned that America had been forced to mature too quickly, sacrificing leisure, art, and poetry for the tasks of national growth. We were too busy taking this land from its native inhabitants and then defending it against other nations to establish American culture; our seeds for originality lay ungerminated. We turned to Europe, with its centuries of creative history, for our art. What resulted were reproductions, weak cuttings for transplanting in an environment unsuited for their nourishment or understanding.

This dependence upon other countries for artistic achievement and the resulting reproductions were of great concern to Stickley. "We are surrounded with the concrete expression of almost every phase of European frivolity, rather than with the effort to set forth what we *are* in America by what we do." His recognition of the inappropriateness of European art in American culture was a major impetus for his philosophical attitudes.

Stickley's trip to the 1900 Paris Exhibition confirmed his bias against reproductions. He saw for the first time European styles as integral parts of their environment with proper historical se-

3-1. Victorian sitting room, New York, 1898. (Museum of the City of New York)

quence, thus serving as true reflections of their period.

For example, European beds had decorative elements such as enclosing draperies and raised platforms, which both protected the occupant from the cold and dampness and isolated the bed from its surroundings, thus defining an area for rest and comfort. This idea of isolation was present in all classes of European society and can be seen in the cupboard beds of Brittany peasants as well as in the great couches of the French monarchs. This treatment of the bed was, in Stickley's view,

a proper style for its period, but when these same elements were applied to contemporary American environments, they became relics of the past, without any relevance to the current mode of life. "The modern bed, on the contrary, should be constructed with a recognition of the necessity of pure air and of the curative power of sunlight."

Upon his return from Europe, Stickley vowed never to be obedient to the public demand for reproduction furniture. Instead, he would strive for faithful production. His early reading of Ruskin and Emerson helped him to form the theories he later termed collectively a "democratic art": ". . . art that holds the mirror up to life and catches its perfect reflection."

In contrast with the reproductions that filled every shop in the early 1900s, Stickley set out to design furniture that would reflect the needs of the American people, not the historic whims of European aristocracy. Stickley believed these needs arose from the democratic form of government and the practical, working-class identity of most Americans. Stickley's new furniture would be created for ". . . the real Americans, deserving the dignity of this name, since they must always provide the brawn and sinew of the nation . . . the great mass of American people hav[ing] moderate incomes with an unusual degree of mental cultivation. . . ."

Stickley felt that art should be of and by the people, stemming from their everyday lives; thus it would be original because of its natural sincerity. He wrote:

When people know that I am making a new kind of furniture now they say to me, "What period will this be?" It perplexes them when I answer, "No period." I have never sought any period in my work. I am satisfied if it expresses what I believe to be progress in furniture making in America. I believe that there are many people . . . who desire in their homes a certain sturdy elegance, good construction, good craftsmanship, beautiful lines, rich and durable furniture. That is what I am seeking in my new work.

Stickley strove to understand the principles of all art and then to apply them to designing furniture that met the needs of the American people. His first step was to reduce the pieces to their simplest form using vertical and horizontal members in a post-and-lintel system. Aware of the ob-

vious primitiveness of this furniture, he then sought some method of enhancement without sacrificing the structural integrity.

Examination of the early Gothic cathedral provided Stickley with the concept of ornament used as structural necessity. Ornamental features such as the flying buttress were also functional, giving strength and support to the architecture. In later Gothic cathedrals, these features exceeded their function as structural supports and became mere applied surface decoration, a characteristic he despised in period furniture: "Applied ornament is a parasite and never fails to absorb the strength of the organism upon which it feeds." Recognizing the danger in decorativeness for its own sake, Stickley turned his efforts to finding a method of revealing existing

structural elements as ornament.

One method he employed was the extension of the mortise-and-tenon joint, previously hidden, through the surface of the furniture. The configuration of the joint was thus ornamental, yet structurally functional. Joinery shown and used both ornamentally and functionally established what Stickley called "structural style."

This structural style embodied Stickley's democratic art. Furniture in the structural style gave the people objects that presented qualities of order, simplicity, harmony, and honesty. When these qualities appear in objects, they have the same positive effect on people as they do when they are possessed by individuals.

Non-structural objects, those whose forms present a chaos of lines which the

3-2. Craftsman sideboard with hammered copper tray and chafing dish, demonstrating Stickley's use of the extended mortise-and-tenon joint as an ornamental feature. (*The Craftsman*)

eye can follow only lazily or hopelessly, should be swept out from the dwelling of the people, since, in the mental world they are the same as volcanoes and earthquakes in the world of matter. They are the creators of disorder and destruction.

From this belief in the influence of material form over mental mood, Stickley synthesized his fundamental aesthetic: ". . . for the single word 'beauty,' there should be substituted 'the beauty of simplicity.' "

Stickley called furniture in the structural style Craftsman furniture because of the close relation of maker to object. This relation apparently stems from the British Arts and Crafts movement's philosophy at first glance. When Stickley defined this relation, however, he emphasized the motive behind the act, the need for the object, as determining the joy of its construction. "It is what we do ourselves, of our own impelling, that is of value to us. . . . Never do a thing unless something definite justifies it. . . . Let your design grow out of necessity."

The British Arts and Crafts movement advocated singular conception and execution; democratic needs were irrelevant. Stickley viewed the design and construction of objects one at a time and totally by hand as costly. This practice thereby catered to an elite group and fostered an eclectic taste, in direct opposition to a democratic art. In his view this fragmented approach to design could only lead to a halt in the growth of aesthetic identity in society. His desire to see well-designed and crafted furniture available to and within the means of most of his countrymen dictated the necessity for its production in some quantity.

"It is written, 'In the sweat of thy brow . . .' but it was never written, 'In the breaking of thine heart shalt thou eat bread.' " Stickley used this quote from Ruskin to illustrate his own feeling that joy in labor is a necessity without which the product of one's labor is an empty reward. Without it the worker passes the hours trading physical effort for monetary gain, looking to the future for a time when prosperity will release him from this bondage.

Stickley felt trading labor for material gain led to products of an impermanent nature, both physically and asthetically. Inherent in his democratic art is the fulfillment of the needs of the people. The basic needs of the people in a working society are timeless; therefore Craftsman furniture, designed to meet those needs, is also timeless. Manufacturers were well aware of this idea; to ensure their prosperity, they continually fought against it by introducing "up-to-date" styles. This struggle for the new look made the impermanent object a poor standard of excellence. In contrast, Stickley's Craftsman furniture was designed

3–3. An example of what Stickley referred to as nonstructural furniture. (*The Craftsman*)

not only for his contemporaries but also for future generations to live with and adapt to their needs; "pieces that would be first of all practical and comfortable, that would last a man's lifetime without being much the worse for wear; the kind of things one could take pride in handing down to one's grandchildren."

Moreover, Craftsman furniture recognized the marriage of hand and machine in its manufacture, while the Arts and Crafts products were based on the celibacy of the hand. In Stickley's words, "The modern trouble lies not with the use of machinery, but with the abuse of it." The structural style and angular lines of Craftsman furniture were Stickley's way of enabling the machine to be both efficient and a vehicle for the expression of beauty. Rather than allowing technology to deprive the workman of the chance to interact with materials, Stickley felt machines in the hand of a skilled craftsman could be used with sensitivity to liberate the worker from purely mechanical hand labor.

. . . Given the real need for production and the fundamental desire for honest self-expression, the machine can be put to all its legitimate uses as an aid to, and a preparation for, the work of the hand, and the result be quite as vital and satisfying as the best work of the hand alone.

This proper use of the machine gives the worker time for careful material selection and surface finishing that the hand alone can give.

Stickley chose oak as the primary material for his furniture. Oak was abundant in American forests (and thus served as an expression of the natural environment of the people), and it had historic use as a strong structural building material (a direct applica-

3-4. Craftsman furniture room setting in use today.

3-5. Another Craftsman interior in the same home.

3-6. Craftsman rocker with rush seat. The structural style and angular lines of Stickley's furniture enabled craftsmen to combine hand and machine labor.(*The Craftsman*)

tion of the theory of structural style). Having chosen his raw material, Stickley developed methods of using it to its full advantage. "Wood is designed to be cut, and metal to be molded; therefore, when the craftsman fails to recognize these separate and distinct methods of treatment he violates the intuitions of taste and the laws of logic."

Stickley's respect for wood dictated that it should never be abused or forced into unnatural states. The simple form of his Craftsman furniture provided the perfect backdrop for displaying the grain pattern with all its inherent beauty. In contrast, highly ornamented furniture would compete with the grain at every turn. By preserving the beauty of the grain and using proper surface finishing, Stickley intended to prevent the overemphasis of structural primitiveness, which he believed was a direct and necessary result of the reformative nature of his structural style.

In reverting to the primitive ideas of articles of household furniture we find simple and even crude lines. These, in accordance with sound, artistic principles, we have preserved; since in architecture—the first of the building arts—the constructive features must be plainly visible and declare the purpose and use of the work.

Surface finishing was another area where Stickley demanded respect for natural materials. Only those finishes that enhanced the natural color, grain, and texture of the wood and did not hide or attempt to imitate qualities of other, more costly woods, were used. In this way the hand and eye would not be isolated or misled in their experience.

Throughout the process of conceiving his Craftsman furniture,

Stickley's intellectual endeavors expanded in directions far beyond his primary concern with furniture design. His theory of democratic art applied to many facets of American life, and he saw its potential power to transform the total environment of the working people. In order to bring art to the people and make it applicable to their everyday lives, he published *The Craftsman*. In it he expounded his philosophy with remarkable skill and sought to inspire the public to incorporate the principles of art into their daily lives. He presented not only his own ideas but those of his contemporaries, bringing the words of philosophical and artistic giants of the day including Auguste Rodin, Irving Gill, Myron Hunt, Leopold Stokowski, Louis Sullivan, and Theodore Roosevelt, to his general readership.

He wrote that schools should provide a balance of theory and manual training inspired by nature, the greatest teacher. He referred to this collective approach as "putting the whole child to school." He felt if the child observed nature's unbiased treatment of the environment (no plant or animal ill-prepared to survive, purely functional yet beautiful), then character would be molded in nature's image; no idea or product would be formed that would not fit the precepts of democratic art. Schools were establishing programs of manual training, prompted by the public's interest in the practicality of their children's education. This interest was more than just the desire that children learn a skill; it also encompassed the moral and mental development of self-discipline, thus assuring strong character and joy in labor.

Stickley clearly saw that when men lacked joy in their labor, their frustrations could lead to crime and violence: ". . . the average adult criminal is not uneducated

3-7. Furniture pieces from a manual training class, Los Angeles, CA. (*The Craftsman*)

3–8. California bungalow built in keeping with Craftsman ideals of architecture.

but unskilled." He suggested that rehabilitation of the criminal could be achieved through meaningful work.

From the structural style of his Craftsman furniture, Stickley developed his ideas for Craftsman architecture. He used the same criteria of natural materials, structural style, and evident joinery to build pleasing homes for working people.

Early in the development of industrial, mechanized society, Stick-ley saw the destructiveness of depersonalization and the need to restore a source of pride and an outlet for originality to the working man. He had great respect for the American public as intelligent, enterprising people and wanted them to practice self-reliance, to seize their unique opportunity to create their own history and art unshackled by class distinction and inappropriate tradition. He provided inspiration to the average person to realize his or her poten-tial and create an environment stripped of artificial trappings—a pure and beautifully simple place to live and work in harmony with nature and mankind.

I did not realize at the time that in making those few pieces of strong, simple furniture, I had started a new movement. Others saw it and prophesied a far-reaching development. To me it was only furniture; to them it was religion. And eventually, it became religion with me as well.

A Selection of Craftsman Furniture

Arm Rocker

No. 311. Arm rocker, rush seat. Height of back from floor, 34 in. (86.36 cm); height of seat from floor, 15 in. (38.10 cm); size of seat, 20 in. (50.80 cm) wide, 19 in. (48.26 cm) deep.

Rocker

No. 305½. Rocker, hard leather seat. Height of back from floor, 31 in. (78.74 cm); height of seat from floor, 14 in. (35.56 cm); size of seat, 16 in. (40.64 cm) wide, 16 in. (40.64 cm) deep.

Side Chair

No. 338. Small chair, with pewter and copper inlays by Harvey Ellis. Height from floor of back, 40 in. (101.60 cm); height of seat from floor, 18 in. (45.72 cm); size of seat, 15 in. (38.10 cm) wide, 14 in. (35.56 cm) deep.

Arm Chair

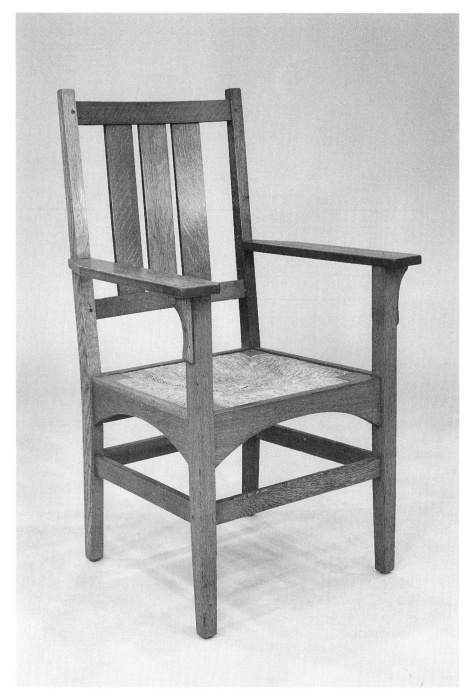

No. 340. Arm chair, rush seat. Height of back from floor, 41 in. (104.14 cm); height of seat from floor, 18 in. (45.72 cm); size of seat, 18 in. (45.72 cm) wide, 16 in. (40.64 cm) deep.

Reclining Chair

No. 369. Reclining chair, adjustable back, spring cushion seat. Height of back from floor, 40 in. (101.6 cm); height of seat from floor, 15 in. (38.10 cm); size of seat, 23 in. (58.42 cm) wide, 27 in. (68.58 cm) deep.

Settle

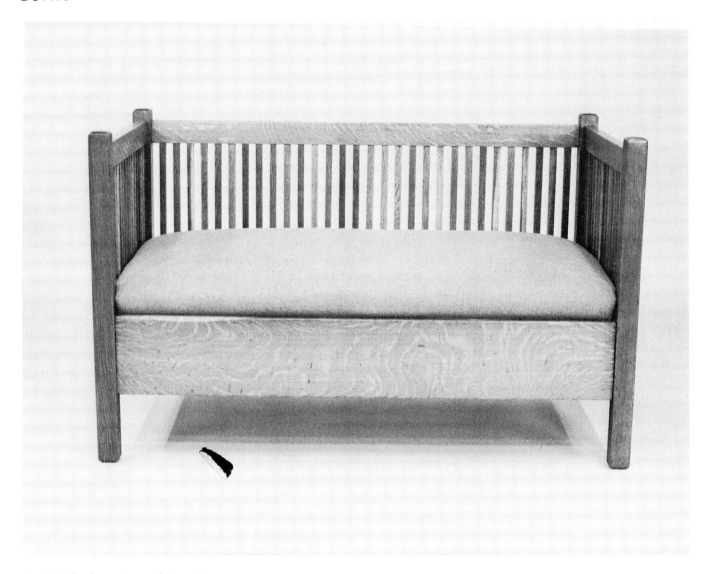

No. 209. Settle, spring cushion cloth seat. Height of back from floor, 31 in. (78.74 cm); height of seat from floor, 18 in. (45.72 cm); size of seat, 50 in. (127.00 cm) long, 28 in. (71.12 cm) deep.

Seat or Footrest

No. 301. Seat or footrest, rush seat. Height of seat from floor, 17 in. (43.18 cm); size of seat, 20 in. (50.80 cm) wide, 16 in. (40.64 cm) deep.

Seat or Footrest

No. 300. Seat or footrest, Craftsman leather. Height of seat from floor, 15 in. (38.10 cm); size of seat, 20 in. (50.80 cm) wide, 16 in. (40.64 cm) deep.

Table

Table with Grueby tile top. Height, 26 in. (66.04 cm); width, 20 in. (50.80 cm); length, 24 in. (60.96 cm).

Taboret

No. 603. Taboret. Height, 20 in. (50.80 cm); diameter, 18 in. (45.72 cm).

Table

No. 607. Table. Height, 29 in. (73.66 cm); diameter, 24 in. (60.96 cm).

Library Table

No. 636. Library table. Height, 29 in.
(73.66 cm); diameter, 48 in. (121.92 cm).

Child's Table

No. 628. Child's table. Height, 22½ in. (57.15 cm); length, 36 in. (91.44 cm); width, 22 in. (55.88 cm).

Lunch Table

No. 647. Lunch table. Height, 30 in. (76.20 cm); length, 40 in. (101.60 cm); width, 28 in. (71.12 cm).

Magazine Cabinet

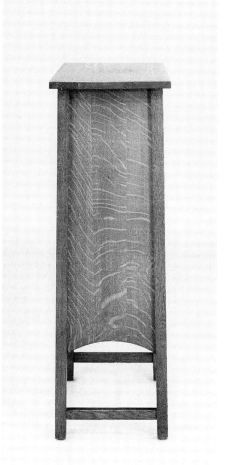

No. 72. Magazine cabinet. Height, 42 in. (106.68 cm); width, 22 in. (55.88 cm); depth, 13 in. (33.02 cm).

China Cabinet

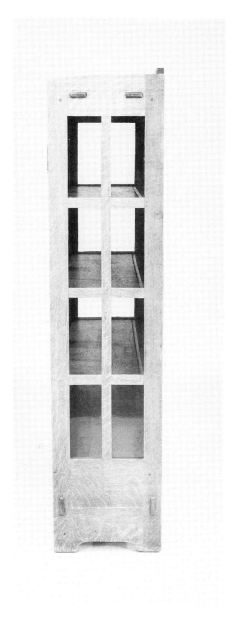

No. 815. China cabinet. Height, 65 in. (165.10 cm); width, 42 in. (106.68 cm); depth, 15 in. (38.10 cm).

Serving Table

No. 818. Serving table. Height, 39 in. (99.06 cm); width, 48 in. (121.92 cm); depth, 20 in. (50.80 cm).

Serving Table

No. 809. Serving table. Height, 40 in. (101.60 cm); width, 54 in. (137.16 cm); depth, 18 in. (45.72 cm).

Library Table and Table Cabinet

No. 615. Library table. Height, 30 in. (76.20 cm); length, 48 in. (121.92 cm), depth, 30 in. (76.20 cm). Table cabinet is 9 in. (22.86 cm) high, 24 in. (60.96 cm) long, and 9 in. (22.86 cm) deep.

Writing Table

No. 720. Writing table. Height, 38 in. (96.52 cm); width, 38 in. (96.52 cm); depth, 21 in. (53.34 cm).

Desk

No. 729. Desk. Height, 43 in. (109.22 cm); width, 36 in. (91.44 cm); depth 14 in. (35.56 cm).

Desk

Desk with reed and raffia basket. Height, 46 in. (116.84 cm); width, 20 in. (50.80 cm); depth, 16 in. (40.64 cm).

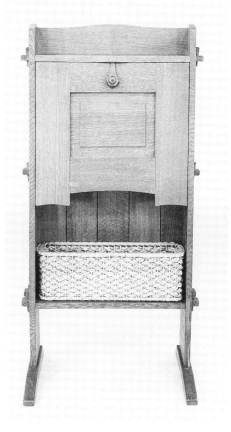

Piano Lamp

Desk Lamp

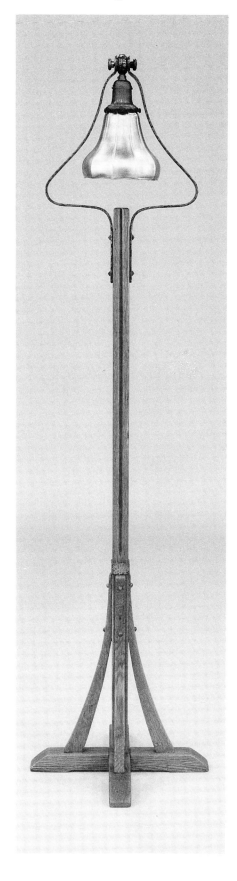

No. 500. Piano lamp, oak standard with hand-wrought copper frame supporting the shade. Height, 60 in. (152.40 cm).

No. 501. One-light electric desk lamp. Height, 16 in. (40.64 cm); width, 8½ in. (21.59 cm).

Hall Mirror

Costumer

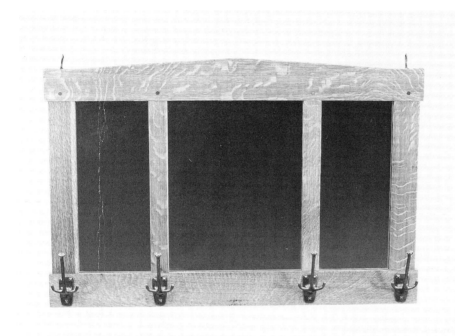

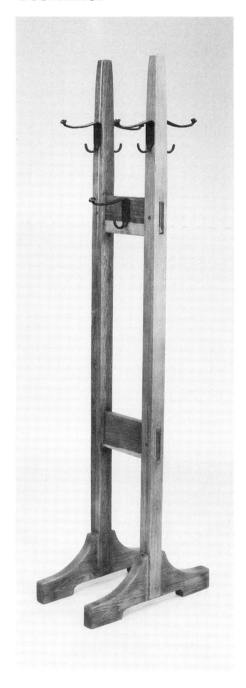

No. 67. Hall mirror. Height, 28 in. (71.12 cm); length, 42 in. (106.68 cm).

No. 53. Costumer. Height, 72 in. (182.88 cm); width, 14 in. (35.56 cm); 6 iron hooks.

Three-Fold Screen

No. 81. Three-fold screen, Craftsman canvas appliquéd with flower motifs in panels. Height, 58 in. (147.32 cm); width, 54 in. (137.16 cm).

4. Materials and Methods

WOOD AND ITS SELECTION

Stickley's Notes on Wood

The world has never found any substitute for wood in its many utilities and its natural beauty. Time and the forces of Nature have wrought out the many wonderful fibers and textures, and the almost endless variety of beautiful traceries in the grains and the interesting age-mark rings which keep the record of the birthdays of the forest trees.

Writers innumerable have expatiated, and justly too, upon the beauty of the trees—the trunk, the branches, the leaves, the shadows they cast and the shelter the branches and leaves afford to the birds. The mystery of the vast forests; even the cutting down of trees, the rafting of them down the streams to the mill, and, eventually, the singing of the saws that divide them into lumber, have been subjects for writings and poems that move and stir the soul. In this article I wish with all earnestness to comment upon the beauty of the trees when cut up into lumber. There is a charm as individualistic and as marked in the wood itself as is that of the trees in the forest. This beauty lies in the grain, or markings; the texture, or surface appearance; the natural shades, or colors; the marvelous varieties in grain and texture; the readiness with which they yield themselves to color treatment, and the results so attained. Many a worker in wood loses much of the joy he might have in his work by not making a study of these beautiful details. Is it not evident that he who loves to look at the wood upon which he is engaged will enjoy his work far more than one who sees no beauty in it? It is to help arouse this joy—that is one of the essential conditions of artistic work—that I wish briefly to comment upon the special beauties certain woods possess, and how

best in the finishing processes to bring these into prominence and retain them.

And, in addition, there exists in wood a quality so satisfying that the proper use of it in the structural features of a house produces an effect of completeness which does away with the need of elaborate furnishings or decoration. I believe that one reason why so many people pile unnecessary furniture, pictures and bric-a-brac into their houses is because the *necessary* furniture, the woodwork (or other treatment) of the walls, and the color scheme as a whole are not interesting enough. This is a point that can hardly be too strongly emphasized in its bearing upon the creation of beautiful and restful surroundings in the home.

If the woodwork of your house is finished so that the natural beauty of the woods is enhanced; if the same thing were done in the furniture; and you then see that the color scheme of woodwork, furniture and hangings harmonize, you cannot fail to secure in each room a charm and beauty that is a great step accomplished towards the simplicity and restfulness that it is so desirable to gain. For let it never be forgotten that if a room is pleasing and restful, one of the highest and best of results has been attained.

In the American Museum of Natural History in New York is one of the largest and finest collections of woods in America, possibly in the world. A variety of trees from all parts of the world is shown, and each specimen, as a rule, consists of a portion of the trunk, just as it grew, a sawed section unpolished, and a section polished. For decades, and in some instances for centuries, these trees have been absorbing from the soil and atmosphere the elements necessary to their life. Slowly, so slowly that the eye alone could not record it, ring by ring has been added to their growth, the proper

coloring matter absorbed, and the particles of which they are composed deposited in never-failing arrangement. Year after year, century after century, the same plan of structure was followed, until now, when a tree is cut down and its texture and color revealed, we find it harmonious with its species, yet individual in its possession of distinctive and personal qualities. It is this personal quality that gives such delight to the observant woodworker. There is absolutely as much difference between the personality of woods as there is in human beings.

This peculiar charm of grain and texture in woods is owing to the way the tree builds up its cell structure. Each tree does this after its own fashion, and wood is called hard, soft, light, heavy, tough, porous, elastic or otherwise according to these cells. All are more or less familiar with the circular rings that appear when the tree is cut down, or as a log is sawed across. These rings or layers are deposited, one each year, on the outside. So it is apparent the oldest portion of the tree is on the inside. This old portion is what is known as the heartwood, and is tougher, heavier, and stronger than the younger wood or sap wood. Growths materially differ in spring and summer, and these differences are marked in the rings. In the Southern pines, for instance, the spring and summer growths are shown by solid bands.

As a rule these cell structures and their corresponding markings are vertical, but there is a lesser system of cells equally inportant to the life of the tree, which extend horizontally. These are the cells that form the peculiar wavy lines seen in quarter-sawn oak, which cross the vertical rays, and are called medullary rays. These transverse rays are what bind the tree together. When one thinks of the hundreds of tons of weight the trunk of a tree is compelled to bear he cannot help wondering at its strength. It is these medullary rays that bind the perpendicular fibers together and give this amazing strength. Were it not for them the tree would "telescope," as we sometimes see in the case of a tree of which the lower part of the trunk has decayed.

All these matters, which at first sight may seem unimportant, have a practical bearing upon the art of cabinet-making. The young worker should know that, owing to the difference in density in the old and new rings, and also in the growth of spring and summer, some woods when cut have a strong tendency to split or "check." Others incline to warp badly, and still others, of softer fiber, if placed where there is much wear will "sliver" and soon present an uneven and unpleasing surface. To avoid this checking, warping and slivering some logs, when cut into boards, instead of being cut the whole width of the trunk are quartered and then sawn, as shown by the lines in the accompanying diagram [see figure 4-1]. This is called quarter sawing. There are woods that, in their very nature, do not warp easily, such as chestnut, pine, and mahogany, etc. These, for general purposes, therefore, are usually plain sawn.

Let us now, for a few moments, consider the question of wood sawing; why the different methods are followed on certain woods, and the objects that are attained.

The quarter-sawing method of cutting oak,—that is, the making of the cut parallel with the medullary rays and thus largely preserving them, instead of cutting across them and thus destroying their binding properties, renders quarter-sawn oak structurally stronger, also finer in grain, and, as before shown, less liable to check and warp than when sawn in any other way.* Its cost, however, is largely increased on account of the greater waste in sawing.

On the other hand plain sawn oak is an entirely different wood. It presents a marked coarseness of texture that relegates its use to purposes that do not demand finer and more pleasing qualities.

*This of course, makes a difference when it comes to making large panels, table tops, or anything else that shows a large plain surface, and for these uses quarter-sawn oak is preferable merely because it "stands" better [Stickley's note].

The long wide markings that are discernible in the accompanying illustrations [figure 4-2] are called "flakes." These are caused by the saw's cutting through the more solid portions of the yearly rings which extend the whole length of the trunk from bottom to top. To make clearer what I mean: If one holds in his hands a piece of wood of any of the kinds named, he can observe by looking at the ends, that these long flakes are portions of the yearly rings exposed by the cut of the saw. To distinguish these perpendicular flakes (that band the whole tree

trunk) from the horizontal medullary "ray flakes," I shall call them "ring flakes"—from the yearly rings that cause them. So that in future when I speak of "ring flakes" and "ray flakes," the qualifying adjective will denote the kind of flakes meant.

When wood is sawn in the ordinary way, that is, with the "lay" of the yearly rings, the wood is called "plain sawn." The ring flake is produced only by plain sawing, while the ray flake is produced only by quarter sawing.

The drying of woods is not a thing to

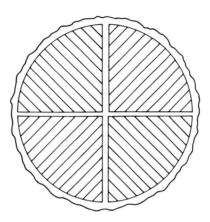

4-1. Quarter-sawing method of cutting boards.

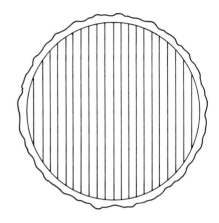

4-3. Plain-sawing method of cutting boards.

4-2. Quarter-sawn white oak.

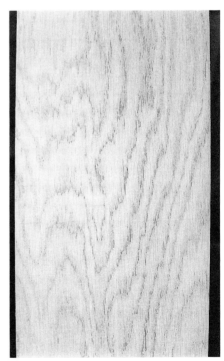

4-4. Plain-sawn white oak.

be attempted unadvisedly or indiscreetly. It demands knowledge, care, experience and constant watching. If the outside of lumber is dried too rapidly it produces what is known as "case-hardening." This is the solidification of the outside so that moisture of the inside is confined. This causes the checking (splitting at the ends) and warping of the wood.

Experience demonstrates that in the first stages of drying, the air should not be too dry. To prevent this in the "dry-kiln" a small jet of steam is injected into the room so as to keep the air slightly moist. If this is properly done and the heat not too great at first the lumber will dry from the inside outwards, instead of on the outside first. This is the whole—or, at least, the chief—secret of the proper drying of woods.

It must not be overlooked, however, that science as yet has discovered no way of overcoming the prior necessity of "air-drying" all lumber before it goes into the kiln. By this is meant the piling of lumber out-of-doors so that the sun-warmed air may get to it and first "season" it before any further artificial drying is attempted. Experimentalists have tried again and again to dispense with this process, on account of the time it consumes, but every attempt to subject "green" wood (wood not yet air-dried) to artificial drying processes has proven a failure, thus demonstrating that in some things, at least, Nature insists upon the observance of her own methods.

Quarter sawn oak is the hardest of all woods to dry, and requires the longest time. The reason for this is that the flat surfaces of the ray flakes being almost as impenetrable as glass prevent the moisture from escaping through them, and therefore it has to come out at the ends and sides. It is obvious how carefully and thoroughly this must be done, and that only men of large experience and trustworthiness can be placed in charge of such responsible work.

To ensure thoroughness all quarter sawn oak is carefully inspected again, after it leaves the dry-kiln, not only to see that it is ready for use, but also for the purpose of selecting the pieces best adapted to certain work, and that match well in color and grain. Woods with beautiful or special markings are set aside for extra fine work, and more ordinary pieces are used for the more ordinary work.

Then saw, chisel, planer and other tools do their work, and, in due time, after the scraper and smoother has done his part, the chair, table or other article is ready for the final coloring process, which heightens, beautifies and renders permanent the texture and traceries bestowed by Nature.

Determining Board Feet

Hardwood is sold in units identified as board feet. A board foot is 12 inches (30.48 cm) wide, 12 inches (30.48 cm) long and 1 inch (2.54 cm) thick, or 144 cubic inches (365.76 cm^3). Hardwood is normally milled in random widths and lengths to maximize the use of each hardwood log. Each board is sawed as wide and long as the log allows and then trimmed just enough to square the ends and edges.

In order to determine the number of board feet in any given piece of furniture, you must convert the dimensions for its parts to cubic inches and then to board feet. When computing the board feet in a selected piece of wood, you measure the piece's length, width, and thickness in inches and, using the following formula, convert the measurements to board feet:

$$\frac{length \times width \times thickness}{144 \text{ cubic inches}} =$$

$$\text{number of board feet}$$

For example, a board 48 inches long, 6 inches wide, and 2 inches thick would be figured as follows:

$$\frac{48 \text{ inches} \times 6 \text{ inches} \times 2 \text{ inches}}{144 \text{ cubic inches}} =$$

$$\frac{576 \text{ cubic inches}}{144 \text{ cubic inches}} =$$

$$4 \text{ board feet}$$

Grading

Hardwood is graded according to the percentage of clear face cuttings, those that are unblemished by knots or other defects, that can be obtained from any selected piece. Hardwood has four grades: FAS (firsts and seconds), Select, #1 Common, and #2 Common.

FAS (firsts and seconds): clear face on both surfaces, yielding approximately 91 percent clear face cuttings. Minimum board widths, 6 inches (15.24 cm); lengths, 8 to 16 feet (2.44 to 4.88 m). FAS is actually a combination of firsts (premium quality boards) and seconds (slightly less perfect boards). These are almost always grouped together under the grade FAS, and one cannot specify only firsts when ordering. FAS lumber is used almost exclusively for furniture construction.

Select: clear face on one surface only, yielding a minimum of 91 percent clear face cuttings. Minimum board widths, 4 inches (10.16 cm); lengths, 6 to 16 feet (1.83 to 4.88 m).

#1 Common: some defects on both surfaces, yielding a minimum of 66 to 75 percent clear face cuttings. Minimum board widths, 3 inches (7.62 cm); lengths, 4 to 16 feet (1.22 to 4.88 m).

#2 Common: many defects on both surfaces, yielding a minimum of 50 to 66 percent clear face cuttings. Minimum board widths, 3 inches (7.62 cm); lengths, 4 to 16 feet (1.22 to 4.88 m).

In choosing a grade of wood for furniture construction, clear face cuttings are essential for visual continuity. When encountering defects such as knots, you should not immediately rule out the use of that section unless the defect makes the board structurally unsound. If the defect is visual in nature, it can sometimes be positioned so as not to detract from the lines of the piece of furniture. This careful selection allows latitude in mixing wood grades.

Ordering

The thickness of hardwood is expressed in quarters of an inch, with the minimum thickness being 4/4 (1 inch [2.54 cm]) for all hardwoods. 8/4 (2 inch [5.08 cm]) and 12/4 (3 inch [7.62 cm]), are also standard thicknesses for hardwood. When ordering wood in the aforementioned quarters, you are expressing a measurement of the board's thickness in its first cut from the log. It still has large saw marks and may contain pieces of bark, making further surface cleaning necessary. The finished piece of lumber will therefore actually be slightly less than the 4/4, or one inch, of its original measurement.

Buying wood in the rough (before final cleaning) and having it surfaced at the lumberyard is less costly than buying surfaced wood at a hardwood specialty shop. On the other hand, buying at a specialty shop allows you to look at the grain pattern of each available board and select those you want. In unsurfaced wood the grain pattern is obscured by the extremely rough surface, and you get a chance selection. Whether you should buy surfaced or unsurfaced wood is a choice that must be made on an individual basis. When ordering unsurfaced stock, it never hurts to request highly figured wood, since the lumberyard will usually try to accommodate you.

Defects

Lumber defects occur in all grades and are categorized according to the following descriptions:

Cupped: a board that is hollow across its width, forming a rounding on its underside. Cupping usually results from incorrect stacking.

Bowed: a board curved along its length so that it rocks on one of its faces. Bowing is usually caused by uneven or too widely placed spacers in stacks.

Sprung or Edge-bent: a board that retains its flatness but bends along its edge plane.

Warped: a board twisted along its length.

Checked: a board that has separated or split along its length. Checking occurs when wood is dried too rapidly or improperly.

Stained: irregular markings that can be caused by wood-rotting fungi, soil conditions, frost factors, chemical contamination, or natural oxidation or weathering.

Methods of dealing with various defects in construction will be discussed in the following sections.

4-5. Lumber defects. Top to bottom: warped, sprung, bowed, cupped.

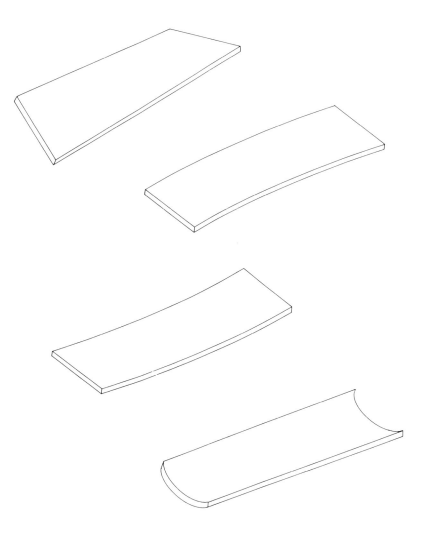

Layout

You should always spread out the boards you have purchased for a project and take note of their size, grain patterns, and defects before cutting. You can then match grain patterns with the proper size and use of each part of the project, and you will use your wood as economically as possible.

To lay out the project, consult the drawing of the project and the materials list and make a series of rough paper patterns of the parts. These rough paper patterns should be ¼ inch (.64 cm) to ½ inch (1.27 cm) wider than finished width and 1 inch (2.54 cm) longer than finished length. Label these patterns with the part name and location (e.g., right front leg) and place these patterns on the boards, keeping in mind any defects in the wood as well as design considerations.

Defects can be grouped into two categories, wood distortions and physical breaks. Cups, bows, springs, and warps are wood distortions and will affect the cutting and fitting of a joint. Physical breaks such as checks and loose knots may affect the structural strength of a board.

A distorted piece of wood can be used if certain procedures are followed. A bowed board can be used when cut into short sections. A cupped board can be used when cut into long, narrow sections. A warped board is difficult to use and must be cut into both short and narrow pieces. Physical breaks, such as severe checks and loose knots, must be cut away. Small checks or secure knots should not affect the soundness of the wood and can be cosmetically filled and carefully positioned.

When placing patterns on the boards, remember that similar parts should have some grain pattern and color in common. Small parts should have small grain markings so as not to have their shape altered visually, while larger parts will accommodate most grain patterns well. Matching grain patterns may lead to a good deal of waste, but the most economical cut may not be visually satisfying. Therefore, each craftsman must strike his own balance between economics and aesthetics. If you chose the wood carefully for each part, you will have a series of parts that form a piece of furniture well balanced in color and grain when finally assembled.

Once the patterns have been positioned, draw around each with a piece of chalk, remove the pattern, and mark each piece of wood with the information from the pattern. Add marks to indicate outside and inside surfaces.

PREPARATION

Once the wood has been marked with rough patterns and labels, you are ready to begin cutting. Before you make any cuts, look at the materials list provided with each project and plan cutting sequences so that pieces of the same length and width can be cut at the same time. This saves time and ensures greater consistency of measurements.

Using a handsaw, a circular saw, or a radial arm saw, rough-cut each board into workable lengths. Now each workable length can be jointed, planed, and cut to width according to the dimensions given in the materials list. To cut pieces to length, square one end and mark it so it is easily identified as the squared end. Then measure from the squared end to the appropriate length for the piece, mark, and cut. To accurately cut several pieces the same length, use a jig: square one end of all matching pieces, and then use the jig to make the final cut to length for each one.

Safety Reminders

The following list contains general safety reminders to protect you and others near you when working with and around tools in the shop.

1. Do not use any tool until you thoroughly understand how it works.
2. Use guards on power equipment. Some operations may require removal of the guard, but additional safety precautions should be used to take the place of the guard (such as using a push stick or jigs, or devising alternative guards as aids to specialized cutting).
3. Always keep loose clothing tucked in, shirt sleeves rolled up, and long hair tied back. Remove all jewelry from hands, wrists, and neck.
4. Wear approved eye protection.
5. Carefully check stock for loose knots, splits, metal objects, and other defects before milling.
6. Keep the floor around work areas clean to prevent slipping and falling. Keep all power tool surfaces clean.
7. Never talk to or interrupt anyone who is working on a machine or turn your attention away from the machine while you are working on it. Keep your eyes focused on the cutting action at all times.
8. Make all adjustments and blade or cutter changes with the power off or disconnected and the machine at a dead stop.

JOINERY

I thus clearly recognized the dangers of applied ornament and advanced a step from which I have never retrograded. I endeavored to turn such structural devices as the mortise and tenon to ornamental use; to employ them in such a way as to force them to give accent and variety to the outlines of the object in which they occurred . . . structural devices such as the mortise and tenon, which, while strengthening the framework and so heightening the serviceability of the object, also emphasize, at the proper points, the outlines presented to the eye.

The mortise-and-tenon joint became to Stickley furniture what the claw foot was to Victorian furniture: a decorative signature. The mortise and tenon is one of the best joints for building furniture because of its superior strength. Its primary function in Craftsman furniture is to join the major frame of each piece (legs to rails, slats to rails, and stretchers to rails). A variety of mortise-and-tenon joints exist in Stickley furniture, including keyed, doweled blind, and doweled through. Each variation uses the basic mortise-and-tenon form explained in the sections that follow.

Tenon Layout and Cutting

Determine the length of the tenon and measure in the appropriate distance from the end of the stock. Using a square, draw a line all the way around the stock. This line defines the shoulders of the tenon. Do this on both ends of the stock. Then check the length of the stock from shoulder to shoulder to make sure the measurement is exactly the same on all faces. This is an important dimension since it will determine the finished size and alignment of the piece of furniture.

Draw lines from the shoulders towards the ends on each face and edge showing the material to be removed. A marking gauge can be used to transfer measurements. Connect these lines to the opposite face or edge across the ends of the stock, forming a square or rectangle on the end surface. If not otherwise specified, the tenon should be about one-half the thickness of the stock.

Use a wide dado blade on a table saw and a miter guide to cut away wood from each face and edge, following these steps:

Using the drawing on the end of the stock as a guide, adjust the blade height to remove material from the lower face. Position the stock with its edge against the miter guide, aligning the shoulder line with the edge of the blade. Cut away material on the down face. Turn the stock over and repeat (figure 4-6).

Slide the shoulder of the stock away from the blade and remove any remaining material on both faces with additional passes (figure 4-7).

Using the drawing on the end of the stock again, adjust the blade height to remove material from the lower edge. Place the stock with its face against the miter guide (clamped if over 24 inches [60.96 cm] long), aligning the previous cut on the face with the blade. Cut away material on the down edge. Turn the stock over and repeat (figure 4-8).

4-6. Align the shoulder line with the edge of the blade and cut material from each face.

4-7. Remove remaining material on both faces.

4-8. Place the face against the miter guide, align the shoulder-line cut with the edge of the blade, and cut material from each edge.

4-9. Finished tenon.

Slide the shoulder of the stock away from the blade and remove any remaining material on both edges with additional passes (figure 4-9).

Cutting Tenons on Bent Stock

In some cases a tenon must be cut on the end of a piece that has been bent. Begin by laying out the angle of the tenon shoulder. Place the bent slat, convex side up, so that it curves over and rests on the two members it will enter. These two members should be lying on a flat surface, spaced as they will be in the finished piece. Draw a pencil line on both edges of the bent slat, using a straight-edge as an extension of the inside face of each member the slat rests upon. Remove the bent slat and draw lines across both faces of it to connect the edge marks.

Draw the tenon on the edges of the slat, perpendicular to the shoulder line using dimensions given for the specific project. Using a backsaw, cut on the shoulder line into the top and bottom faces to the tenon drawn on the edge.

4-11. Cutting a dado to the desired depth and width.

Then, using a bandsaw, cut in from the end along the top and bottom of the tenon until you meet the shoulder cuts you made in each face.

Measure and mark the width of the tenon on the tenon faces and on the end according to the dimensions given for the specific project (figure 4-10). Cut into both edges of the tenon 1/16 inch (.15 cm) away from the shoulder line on the tenon side, using a back-

saw. Continue this cut until you reach your tenon width line. Using the backsaw, cut in from the end on both tenon width lines until you reach your previous cut.

Remove the 1/16 inch (.15 cm) of material to the shoulder lines on the edge of the stock. Use a flat chisel, removing a little material at a time, until you have a smooth, even shoulder.

Barefaced Tenons

Set the dado blade of a table saw to cut to the appropriate depth, and clamp a stop on the miter guide to remove the required material from the end of the stock. Cut with the face of the stock resting on the table (figures 4-11 and 4-12). Reset the dado blade of the table saw to cut the

opposite face to the appropriate depth, and reclamp the stop on the miter guide to remove the required material from the same end. This time, cut with the back

4-12. Finished dado in end of stock.

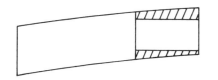

4-10. Blind tenon for bent back slats. Shaded area indicates waste material.

of the rail resting on the table (figure 4-13). With the blade and miter guide stop in the same positions, place the face against the miter guide and make the final tenon cut (figures 4-14, 4-15, and 4-16).

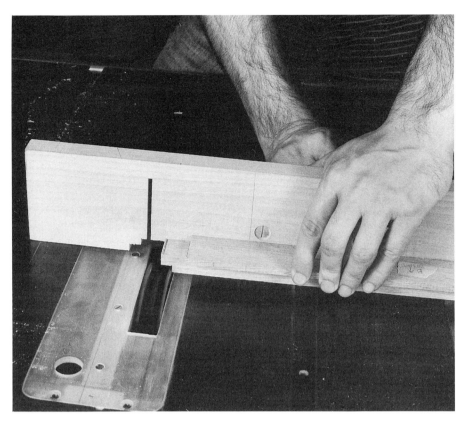

4-13. Cutting a barefaced tenon onto the stock.

4-15. Outside view of the finished barefaced tenon.

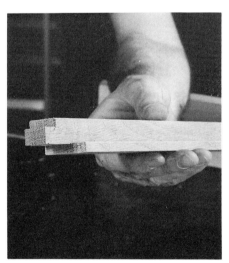

4-16. Inside view of the finished barefaced tenon.

4-14. Cutting the shoulder of the barefaced tenon.

Mortise Layout and Cutting

Determine whether the tenon that fits into the mortise is blind or through, and find the proper face or edge of entry and exit (exit for through tenons only). Mark the dimensions of the tenon on the stock at the entry and exit points. You should now have a square or rectangular drawing showing where the mortise will be cut. Proceed with cutting, following the instructions below. (The mortise shown is for a key in a tenon. The cutting procedure is the same for any mortise in any part.)

Mark the center points of the mortise as guides for drilling (figure 4-17).

To remove excess material in the center of the mortise, use a drill bit that is not larger than the width of the mortise. Drill a series of holes to the desired depth (figure 4-18). When drilling through mortises, place a piece of wood under the stock to prevent splintering when the drill exits, and drill completely through the stock.

Using a sharp, flat chisel with the bevel facing in, gently incise the mortise perimeter until you have a cleanly defined opening. Remove remaining material, working out to the previously marked lines on all sides (figure 4-19).

When both mortise and tenon have been cut, some additional adjustments are usually required for proper fitting of the joint. A well-fitted joint is one that can be assembled with hand pressure but is not so loose that it falls apart by itself. If a joint must be trimmed, always remove material from the piece that fits into the second member. Trim the tenon, for example, not the mortise.

Chalk can be used to locate areas on the tenon that need trimming. Rub the chalk over the interior surface of the mortise, and slide the tenon with hand pressure into the mortise until it stops. Remove the tenon and check its surface for chalk marks, which indicate areas to be trimmed. Remove excess wood gradually with a flat chisel. Check the fit by inserting the tenon into the mortise again. Continue to refine the joint by repeating the above procedure until a perfect fit is achieved and the shoulder of the tenon cleanly meets the surface of the opposing piece.

When the fitting of the mortise and tenon is complete, mark each piece of the joint with a pencil using the same number or letter. This allows quick and accurate identification during assembly.

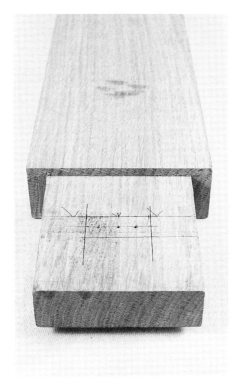

4-17. Mark the center points on the mortise.

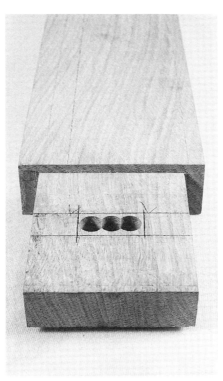

4-18. Drill holes into the mortise to remove center material. Use the center points as drilling guides.

4-19. Remove remaining material with a sharp, flat chisel.

4-20. Cutting a beveled edge by hand, using an angled block of wood as a guide.

4-21. Cutting a beveled edge with a disc sander.

Beveling

Through tenon ends should be beveled to prevent splitting and to cut down the visual harshness of the tenon's projection. Two methods can be used for beveling.

1. Using a block of wood that has been cut at the desired bevel angle (indicated for each project), align and clamp the block to the end of the tenon as shown in figure 4-20. Using the block as a guide, plane the tenon end with a hand plane so that its bevel is the same as the angle cut on the guide block. Move the block and reclamp on the opposite face, then plane that face as well. The edges of the tenon can be beveled without using the guide block by working toward the end. Never plane across the grain.

2. Clamp a straight , clean piece of wood to the table of a disc sander at the desired bevel angle, forming a jig. Slide the tenon end into the disc, keeping it flush to the jig and table surface and cut until the desired depth is reached (figure 4-21). Repeat this procedure on all sides of the tenon end. *Note:* Be sure that you are sanding on the down stroke of the disc sander to prevent the stock from lifting off the table.

Dowels

Many types of joints are strengthened by the insertion of dowels. Stickley used the dowel to strengthen the mortise-and-tenon joint and to butt-join larger pieces edge-to-edge. In the mortise-and-tenon joint, the dowel passes through both the mortise and the tenon, preventing the tenon from backing out of its mortise. The end of the dowel is left exposed on the mortise stock and operates like the exposed tenon as a decorative signature. The use of dowels to pin mortise-and-tenon joints is one of the final steps in construction and is discussed in detail in the assembly section.

Dowel rods are made from many woods, the most common being birch. For the Stickley furniture described in this book, oak doweling has been chosen to complement the wood used in construction. Doweling can be purchased in diameters from ⅛ to 1 inch (.32 to 2.54 cm) in 3-foot (.91-m) lengths.

Butt Joints

To butt-join two pieces edge-to-edge, as for tabletops, wide shelves, and sides, locate the positions of the dowel holes on the two edges that are to be joined. To do this, lay the two rough-cut pieces of stock edge-to-edge as they will be in the finished piece and mark the location of the dowels on both faces. After marking the faces, separate the two pieces, and with a square, transfer the lines to the edge of each piece. With a marking gauge set at one-half the thickness of the stock, mark a line along the length of the edge, intersecting the other lines. This line indicates the centers of each dowel hole. (This step is unnecessary when using a doweling jig.)

4-22. Drilling dowel holes with a self-centering doweling jig.

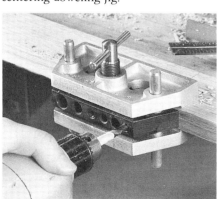

In selecting a dowel size for butt joints, a general rule to follow is that the diameter of the dowel should be not more than one-half the thickness of the stock. The length of the dowel should always be about ¼ inch (.64 cm) shorter than the total depth of the two holes into which it will fit. The ends of the dowels should be beveled, to ease the movement into the hole, and grooved, to allow glue retention and eliminate air pockets that prevent complete insertion of the dowel. Pregrooved and beveled dowels can be purchased in various lengths and diameters for this purpose.

A self-centering doweling jig can be used for locating the position of the holes and guiding the drill bit accurately for boring. This jig has several guide holes for bits of different diameters. It is clamped over the edge of the stock and aligned with the cross line (figure 4-22). Follow instructions provided with the jig to ensure its accuracy.

A piece of masking tape wrapped around the drill bit can serve as a depth indicator. After drilling the holes, try the dowel for fit. It should fit snugly but should be removable by hand. You can sand the dowel for a snug fit.

4-23. Dowels can be spaced at 6-, 8-, or 10-in. (15.24-, 20.32-, or 25.40-cm) intervals.

VENEER

Stickley did not use veneer extensively. He used it to cover visible seam lines in small surfaces, such as table legs, caused by the lamination of several pieces of wood. He also veneered laminated cores in expansive door fronts in drop-front desks and large sideboards needing stability from warping and splitting. He found it necessary to cover these seams and core constructions because they disrupted the visual proportion of that face and thereby detracted from the unity of the piece.

Three of the projects in this book require leg veneers; the following instructions can be used in cutting veneer for each.

First, select a straight piece of 4/4 stock with a definite flake pattern. Cut the stock to width, ½ inch (1.27 cm) larger than the face of the leg to which it will be glued. Mark the face of the stock that is to be the outside of the veneer with an X. Set the fence ⅛ inch (.32 cm) away from the fence side of the blade. Set the blade depth to cut no more than ¾ inch (1.91 cm) with each pass, to prevent burning and binding.

Place the X face against the fence, and pass the stock through the saw. Put the opposite edge down with the X face against the fence, and pass the stock over the blade. Raise the blade (no more than ¾ inch [1.91 cm]) and repeat on both edges. Continue turning,

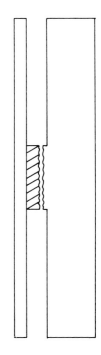

4-24. Veneer cut. Shaded area is planed away.

4-25. Apply glue to veneer strips and leg sides with a small paint roller.

4-27. Place softwood pads between veneer and clamps to prevent denting. Apply clamps alternately, beginning from the center and moving out in both directions.

4-26. Tack each end of the veneer strips with a small brad to prevent slipping when clamp pressure is applied.

cutting and raising the blade until you have ½ inch (1.27 cm) of wood connecting the veneer to the original stock. You do not want to cut the veneer completely away from the stock on the table saw, because the veneer or the stock may fall into the blade.

To separate the veneer, use a handsaw or a band saw and cut down the center of the connecting strip. Then, using either a small hand plane or a planer, remove the remains of the connection from the back face of the veneer (figure 4-24). The veneer is now ready for gluing to the face of the leg.

Apply glue to the veneer strips and leg sides with a small paint roller (figure 4-25). Place the veneer strips on each side to cover the seams, and tack each end of the veneer strips with a small brad to prevent slipping when clamp pressure is applied (figure 4-26). Before clamping, place pine pads between the veneer and clamps to prevent denting. Apply clamps alternately, beginning from the center and moving out in both directions (figure 4-27).

THE ROUTER

The portable router is a versatile tool used for small, accurate milling operations. It consists of an electric motor with a vertical shaft. On the end of the shaft is a collet-type chuck that is designed to hold various-shaped cutting bits, the most durable being carbide. Many people use the router to do decorative molding or edge trimming. Since Stickley furniture has no decorative edgework, we have limited the use of the router to cutting small mortises, beveling panel edges, cutting dados, trimming tabletops, and doing specialized joint work. The router can be used freehand, against a guide or fence, or mounted upside down in a table.

When laminating several boards edge-to-edge for making tabletops or wide shelves, the uneven ends must be trimmed after assembly. This unevenness results when the grains of the different boards are matched. End-trimming after lamination assures an exact end cut for the entire piece. (The trim material has been allowed for in the initial rough length cut of each piece.)

Because the cut necessary to trim such large pieces is so long, table saws, circular saws, and jig-saws give unsatisfactory results. We found the best solution to this problem was to use a router for trimming.

Draw a cutoff line, perpendicular to the edge, at one end. Measure the desired distance from this

4-28. Trimming the end with a router. The router base plate moves along the fence (hidden by right arm), aligning the bit with the pencil cutoff line.

4-29. End after one trimming pass with the router, showing fence clamped in place.

line toward the other end. Draw a second cutoff line perpendicular to the edge at this point.

Clamp a fence or guide parallel to the cutoff line so that when the base plate of the router moves against the fence, the bit edge closest to the fence aligns with the cutoff line. Cut to gradually increasing depths to ensure accurate results. Use a ½- to ¾-inch (1.27- to 1.91-cm) straight bit. Depending upon the type of router you have, you may have to repeat the trim procedure from the opposite face to trim thick stock.

The Router Table

By mounting the router in a table, you can perform some of the operations of a more expensive piece of machinery, the shaper. The construction of a router table is explained here for those who would like to take advantage of its capabilities.

Construct a box with two open sides. The top should be a piece of ½- to ¾-inch-thick (1.27- to 1.91-cm) particle board or birch plywood. Laminate a piece of dull-surface plastic laminant material such as Formica or ⅛-inch (.32-cm) tempered masonite (roughed gently with #220 sandpaper) to the particle board or plywood. Mount the router upside down underneath the top with its base plate countersunk into the underside of the table top (figure 4-30). The chuck extends through a 1-inch (2.54-cm) hole drilled in the tabletop. Countersinking the base plate allows maximum bit extension through the tabletop. The router is held in position under the table by machine screws with heads countersunk into the upper side of the tabletop to give a smooth working surface.

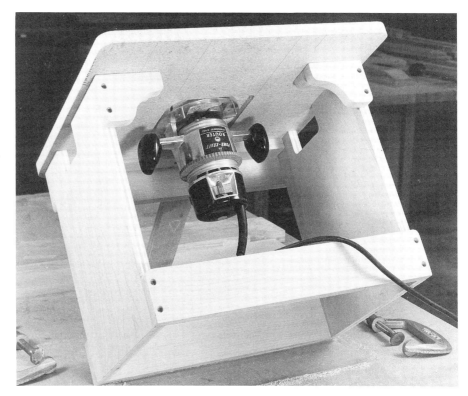

4-30. Router mounted to the underside of a router table. Note countersunk base plate.

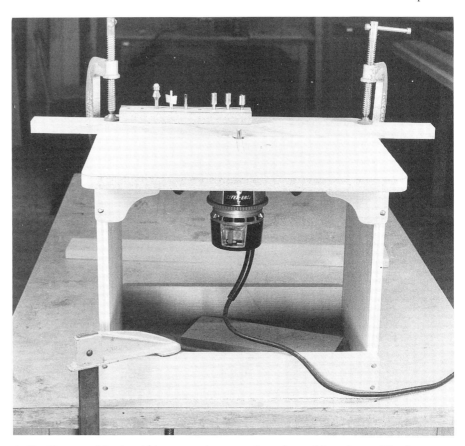

4-31. Router table should be secured to a work surface with a clamp. The fence or guide should also be clamped in position.

When using the router table, a fence or guide is necessary to maintain control and consistency in cutting. The fence should be made of clean, straight stock and clamped to the table as shown in figure 4-31.

When cutting, feed against the rotation of the bit. Your judgment on how fast to feed will have to be a factor of material and experience. The router operates at high speed when not under a load and depends on this speed for accurate cutting. The motor will slow down during cutting. This is normal, but feeding too fast will slow the motor down too much, causing a poor cut. Feeding too slowly overheats the bit, possibly drawing temper from the cutting edge and/or burning the wood.

4-32. Stock is ready to have mortise cut into it. X areas indicate where cuts will be made. Left bit guideline on router table aligns with left mortise end line.

One application for the router with table is cutting mortises.

1. Mark the face of stock to be mortised with lines indicating length and position of the mortise.
2. With a square, transfer the marks to the edge to be mortised. If several mortises are to be cut in a single piece of stock, it helps to mark an X on the face between the endpoint lines of each mortise for easy identification of the areas to be cut (figure 4-32).
3. Set up a fence or guide at the proper distance behind the bit so that when the face of the stock is placed against the fence and brought down slowly on the bit, it will cut a mortise in the *center* of the edge.
4. Draw two parallel lines on the table perpendicular to the fence to indicate the width of the cut the bit will make.

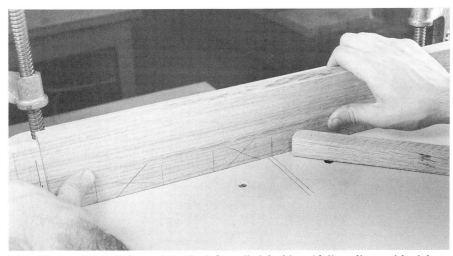

4-33. To cut, slowly slide stock to the left until right bit guideline aligns with right mortise end line.

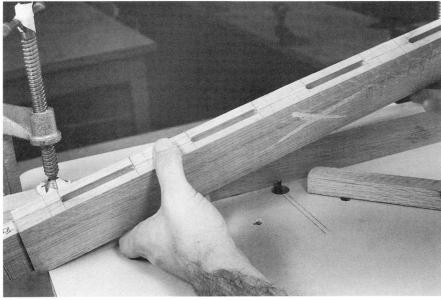

4-34. Finished mortise.

These lines are used to stop and start your cut at the desired points.

5. Clamp a small piece of stock with one rounded corner to the table as shown. This piece keeps the stock firmly positioned against the fence, and its rounded end prevents binding.

6. To prevent inaccurate or burned and chipped cuts, the mortise should be cut in several passes of increasing bit depth. Use a straight bit the width of the mortise. To begin your cut, place the stock against the fence, gradually lower it, watching your guidelines on the face of the wood and the top of the table. Align the left mortise end line with the left bit-width line on the table.

7. Slowly slide the stock to the left, stopping when the right mortise end line is aligned with the right bit-width line (figure 4-33).

8. Slowly slide the stock to your right until the two bit-width lines are centered between the mortise end lines.

9. Slowly lift the stock, pivoting on one end, until it clears the bit.

10. Inspect the mortise for proper length, depth, and cleanness of cut. Refine as necessary (figure 4-34).

The router table can also be used for more specialized cuts. These cutting procedures will be discussed in connection with the projects where they are used.

BENDING

In Stickley furniture, bending is used primarily for chair backs and rockers.

All the rockers now used on Craftsman rocking chairs are cut straight with the grain of the wood and then bent with steam pressure by bending machines. This precaution makes the rocker as strong as any other part of the chair and entirely does away with the danger of breaking that exists when the rocker is cut on a curve that partly crosses the grain.

You can use either of two methods to bend wood: steam bending or immersing the wood in boiling water. Both methods introduce moisture to the wood, partially re-turning the elasticity that the wood had prior to kiln- or air-drying. In this moisture-laden state, the wood can be bent to a desired curve and, if allowed to dry in that position, will permanently retain the arc. The best method to use depends upon your requirements. Steam bending requires less steaming time (approximately one hour of time for each inch of thickness), but you must build a steaming chamber, which could be impractical for just a few pieces. Immersion in boiling water requires an extended soaking period of five to seven hours (depending on thickness), but the equipment needed is minimal and economical for several pieces.

4–35. Mold shown in clamps, with piece to be bent in position. Remember to place clamps spanning the top of the mold once the piece to be bent is in position.

77

The actual bending process for both steaming and immersion is the same. A mold is used to form the wood when it becomes elastic. To make a mold, glue and nail enough pieces of plywood together to form a stack that is at least 1 inch (2.54 cm) wider than the piece to be bent. Draw an arc, using the radius measurement given in the materials list, across the center of the top face of the mold. The radius given for each project part will be less than the finished radius. This allows for partial recovery of the bent part during drying. Cut along this line as accurately as possible with a band saw. Line the curves of both halves of the mold with poster board to keep saw marks from embossing the face of the stock being bent.

To begin bending, place the mold on a set of evenly spaced clamps (see figure 4-35) and insert the soaked or steamed stock. Tighten the clamps alternately so that even pressure is applied on all surfaces. After the bottom clamps are partially tightened, place additional clamps over the top of the mold in between the bottom clamps. Tighten these alternately to completely close the two halves of the mold. *If, at any time during the tightening, you hear any cracking sound, loosen the clamps alternately to evenly reduce tension, and continue steaming or immersion.* Allow the wood to remain in the mold for twenty-four hours. *When removing the clamps, remember to release the tension gradually, alternating clamps for even release.*

SURFACE PREPARATION

After all pieces are cut and their joints are properly fitted, you are ready to prepare surfaces for finishing. The first step is to check each piece, noting any surface irregularities such as dents, minor checks, small open knots, or wormholes.

Small dents can be removed with a household steam iron and a piece of white cotton cloth. Dampen the cloth and place it over the dent. Rub the hot iron lightly over the cloth, forcing the steam to penetrate the cells of the dented area. As the cloth dries, it will need to be redampened. Through repeated applications of steam, the cells will regain their suppleness; the trapped steam will expand them to remove the dent. This process will probably raise the dent above the surrounding wood. Sand the surface level when it is completely dry.

Minor surface checks, small open knots, and wormholes should be filled. Many filling materials are available, but most of them do not match the color and texture of surrounding wood. We obtain the best results with lacquer or shellac sticks or fine sawdust and quick-drying epoxy resin glue.

Lacquer and shellac sticks are available in many tints, enabling close color matches. The stick material is applied to the area to be filled with a small electric soldering iron or a small spatula heated by an alcohol lamp. The heated filler is forced into or glazed over the imperfection and allowed to harden for later sanding.

Epoxy resin glue and sawdust produce a surface quite similar in appearance to that produced by a lacquer or shellac stick. With the epoxy and sawdust method, the color variations result from mixing the epoxy with sawdust from different pieces of wood. (Always use sawdust gathered from sanding with #220 or #320 sandpaper.) Mix epoxy glue according to package instructions; then slowly add sawdust until a sticky, pastelike mixture is obtained. With a small spatula, force this mixture into deep holes and checks. When the surface is dry, it must be sanded level.

Sanding removes any remaining marks on the wood. Four types of sandpaper are used in woodworking.

Flint paper: a grayish material made of soft sandstone, flint paper is good only for simple hand sanding. It has a short sanding life.

Garnet paper: coated with garnet, a reddish brown, hard, natural mineral, garnet paper is excellent for hand sanding and for some power sanding.

Aluminum oxide paper: electrically coated with synthetic abrasive that is either reddish brown or white, aluminum oxide paper is used almost exclusively in commercial furniture making. It is excellent for both hand and power sanding.

Silicon carbide paper: electrically coated with a black, synthetic abrasive, silicon carbide paper is harder and sharper than aluminum oxide but not as tough. It is best therefore to work with light pressure. In the woodworking field, this abrasive is most often used for finish coat sanding.

We chose to use aluminum oxide paper for the projects in this book because of its durability and fast cutting qualities. Though it is more expensive than some other types, it lasts longer under hard use and therefore is just as economical.

All types of sandpaper are graded according to the coarseness of their surface. Two numerical methods grade abrasives; a third method grades papers using descriptive terms such as coarse, medium, or fine. The most precise of these three methods is called the grit number system. In this system each grade is given a number according to the smallest opening through which the abrasive particles will pass. For instance, abrasive particles that will pass through a screen with 100 openings per linear inch (but not through the next smallest screen) are given a grit number of 100. This system ranges from grades of 12 to 600. The second numerical system, called the zero grade system, also uses numbers to indicate abrasive sizes, but it is not as commonly used. For the purposes of this book, references to sandpaper will therefore use the grit number system.

Sanding should be done with a combination of a hand sanding block and an electric orbital sander. Always remember to sand in the direction of the grain. Burn marks, tool marks, and natural grain roughness should be removed by starting with #50 grit paper and progressing in order through the following grades: #80, #100, #120 and #220. Brush the surface to remove all residue before moving to the next finest grade of paper.

When sanding, secure the piece you are working on with a clamp and a softwood pad to prevent damage from the jaw of the clamp. When you are finished sanding with #220 paper, use a short natural bristle brush to buff the surface clean. This final brushing burnishes the wood surface to a smooth, soft luster, eliminating the need for finer finish sanding.

All corners and edges should be softened by sanding with #220 paper until the sharp edge disappears. This treatment of corners and edges is typical of all Stickley furniture and is but another indication of Stickley's attention to the comfort and longevity of his Craftsman furniture.

When all surfaces, edges, and corners have been sanded and the final brushing has been completed, the furniture is ready for assembly.

ASSEMBLY

Clamps

Clamps are used to apply pressure to joints during assembly. Enough clamps must be used along a seamline to give uniform pressure. Clamps should be tightened evenly and to a point where they exert about 150 pounds of pressure per square inch (68.04 kg per square cm). Usually, tightening with one hand will apply the proper pressure. Overtightening will squeeze too much glue from the joint, thus weakening it, or can cause bowing or twisting, thus misaligning the pieces.

Many kinds of clamps are available. We have listed those we feel work satisfactorily for the projects in this book (figure 4-36).

Sliding head bar clamp: widely used in place of C-clamps because of instant adjustment to working size. A multiple-disc clutch allows for quick adjustments.

Fixed head bar clamp: also called cabinet or furniture clamp. Available in lengths from 12 to 76 inches (30.48 to 193.04 cm). A multiple-disc clutch for adjustment is on the tail instead of the head.

Pipe clamp: similar to a fixed head bar clamp, but uses ½- or ¾-inch (1.27- or 1.91-cm) steel pipe in place of the bar. Head and tail fixtures are purchased separately and installed on standard ½- or ¾-inch (1.27- or 1.91-cm) steel pipe. A disadvantage of the pipe clamp is that the pipe flexes more easily than the bar in the bar clamp.

C-Clamp: the name C-clamp is derived from the C shape of the clamp. It is a fixed head-and-tail clamp; therefore, adjustment is slower and its use is limited to small clamping operations. The depth of the throat limits use of the C-clamp to edge clamping.

Adjustable hand screws: made of maple, these are good for clamping irregular shapes that result from two handscrew adjustments. They have broad wooden jaws, reducing the tendency to mar work and cause twisting and slipping.

Band or strap clamp: a nylon band clamps irregular shapes and simultaneously draws together several joints, as when gluing chair stretchers and rails. These clamps are available in several lengths. The band is wrapped around the work and tightened by means of a ratchet. The amount of pressure that can be exerted is limited.

When using any of the above clamps, pads placed between the clamp and your work are necessary to prevent damage. You can use small softwood blocks or attach heavy leather pieces to the clamp with contact cement to form permanent pads.

Dry-Clamping

After selecting the proper size and type of clamp, the next step in assembly is called dry-clamping. This involves putting together all parts or subassemblies without glue. Clamps are positioned and tightened as if each piece were actually being glued. Each joint's fit and proper relationship to surrounding parts is checked at this point. If there are problems with joint fit or alignment, moving the position of the clamp will sometimes cause the joint to shift to its proper alignment. If clamp movements do not remedy the situation, disassembly and some surface cutting or sanding may be necessary to align the joint. After adjustment, dry-clamp the joint again and check alignment. Repeat this procedure until proper fit is achieved. When all joints fit properly when dry-clamped, mark the position of each clamp on the wood with a small piece of masking tape.

Disassemble, removing the clamps so that each can be easily matched with its particular location on the wood again. This will eliminate any major clamp size adjustments when gluing. You are now ready for the final assembly and gluing.

For some projects, gluing and final assembly must be done in a series of steps or subassemblies. Determine which parts require subassembly, and glue and clamp these first. The final assembly steps will be to glue and clamp the subassembled units together.

When assembling or laminating pieces edge-to-edge, dry-clamp by alternating bar clamps under and over the surface to equalize pressure as illustrated in figure 4-37. Use a straightedge laid across both boards (perpendicular to the seam) to check for bowing because of unequal clamp pressure. Adjust clamps until the boards are level and the straightedge lies flush across both boards. If bowing cannot be corrected by clamp adjustment, it may be caused by poor dowel fit or alignment or by a cup in one of the boards. Correct as necessary by sanding, jointing, or planing. Dry-clamp again until a satisfactory fit and level surface are achieved.

Glue Selection and Procedure

Selecting a glue for furniture involves considerations of strength, elasticity, working time, and sanding characteristics. The glue should be strong enough to bear stress loads applicable to the piece (a chair, for example, must bear more stress than a screen or mirror). The glue must have elasticity to accommodate the expansion and contraction of the wood. Working time must be long enough to allow for minor adjustments during final clamping, and the glue, when dry, must be able to be sanded without breaking down.

Stickley used a hide glue in the assembly of Craftsman furniture, since it offered strength and elasticity and was commonly used during his time. Technology has since developed new adhesives that are

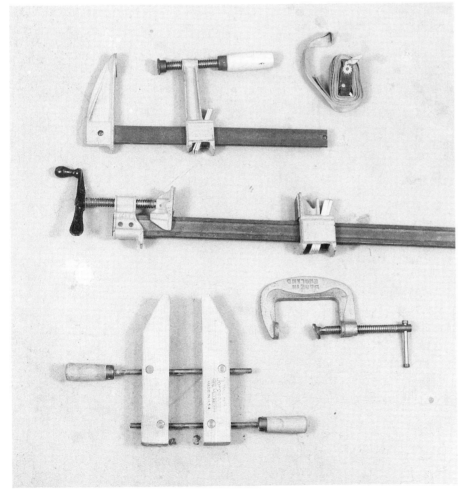

4-36. Clamps. Top to bottom: sliding head bar, strap, fixed head bar, hand screw, and C-clamp.

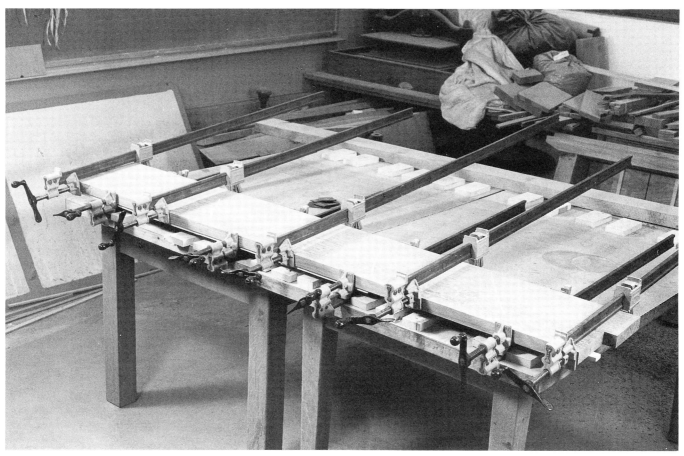

4–37. Bar clamps alternated to equalize pressure on laminated boards.

more practical for the woodworker today. We have chosen to use aliphatic resin glue because it meets all the above requirements and additionally requires short clamping time, dries clear, and cleans up with warm water. This glue should not be confused with polyvinyl acetate (white or Elmer's glue), which is a wood glue with different properties. The aliphatic resin glue is harder and more elastic when dry and therefore superior for the purposes of the projects herein.

Before applying glue to any of the parts, collect the following items: a container of warm water; some clean, white, cotton rags; a variety of sizes of brushes; and an old, flat chisel or metal scraper. These will be used to apply and clean off excess glue that is

squeezed out from joints as they close. You will also need a rubber or rawhide mallet and some scrap pieces of pine.

Apply glue with a brush of an appropriate size to all surfaces of both parts of each joint. Assemble all pieces with hand pressure. Bring the clamps back to their positions and begin to tighten. If any joint should slip out of position, the mallet and a block of pine can be used to tap it back into alignment. Finish tightening clamps, using an alternating pattern to equalize pressure.

For edge-to-edge joining, position the bottom row of clamps and lay several strips of wood (all the same thickness) across the clamps to cushion the stock and prevent staining. (Stains can result when the glue comes in contact

with the wood and the steel clamps.) With the bottom clamps ready, apply glue to the dowels, dowel holes, and both edges of the stock. Insert the dowels into one of the boards. Set the board on edge, dowels extending upward, and lower the second board onto the upright dowels until it meets the first board. Carefully set the two joined pieces onto the clamps; tighten them just to bring the pads into position. Add the top clamps and tighten alternately to equalize pressure.

Cleaning Up

Some excess glue will squeeze from the joint and need to be removed. Using an old chisel or scraper, gently remove the excess glue. Wipe the seam with a damp rag, making sure to remove all glue residue. If any glue is left around the seam, it will seal the surface and cause spots when the finish is applied.

After the appropriate drying time (check manufacturer's instructions on the glue container), remove the clamps in reverse order of their application. Remember to release pressure evenly from clamp to clamp.

The water used to clean around the joints will probably raise or roughen the grain slightly. These areas will need spot sanding, starting with #120 paper and progressing to #220, and brush burnishing. When all joints have been glued, assembly is complete and the piece is ready for finishing.

Glides

Before the final finishing steps, you may wish to add glides to protect the legs of your project from chipping. We suggest the use of Teflon glides with self-contained nails. They can be purchased at most hardware stores and should be attached at this point in the finishing process.

Dowel-Pinning Mortise and Tenon

To pin a mortise-and-tenon joint with a dowel, locate a center point on the surface of the mortised member. This center point will vary with each application of the joint, and more specific location information will be given for each project. After the center point is located, choose the proper bit size and mark the bit with tape to indicate depth.

1. Clamp a block of wood perpendicular to the face where the dowel will enter. Draw lines on this block to serve as vertical alignment guides in one plane (figure 4-38). Pressure against the block itself will provide vertical alignment in the opposite plane.

2. Drill a hole, maintaining vertical alignment with the block and its lines, through one face of the mortised piece, through the tenon, and halfway through the remaining stock toward the opposite face (figure 4-39).

4-38. Guidelines on block of wood clamped to mortised member will maintain vertical alignment when drilling dowel hole.

3. Cut a dowel at least ½ inch (1.27 cm) longer than the depth of the hole and fit it. Apply glue to the inside of the hole and to the dowel. Using a rawhide mallet or a soft pine block and hammer, drive the dowel into place. Wipe the excess glue off with a damp rag.

4. Soak the dowel with water by squeezing a few drops of water on the exposed end; the dowel will swell into its hole for a tighter fit. After a few minutes, wipe off the excess water with a rag and let the surfaces dry.

5. Pad the area around the dowel, as shown in figure 4-40, using three or four layers of masking tape. This pad will prevent the saw from marking the surface when cutting off the dowel. With a coping saw or backsaw, cut off the dowel, leaving a ¹⁄₁₆-inch (.15-cm) projection. Remove the masking tape in one piece (this tape can be used for two or three more dowel trimmings if handled carefully).

6. Sand the dowel flush.

4-39. Drill dowel hole through upper mortised face, tenon, and halfway to lower mortised face.

4-40. With masking tape in place to protect the surface, saw off the dowel.

FINISHING

Finishing was of such importance to Stickley that he was still experimenting with new formulas and methods of application during the later years of his life. In building the projects for this book, we have tried to follow as closely as possible the methods he used in order to maintain the integrity of his designs. In accordance with this, we believe the best expression of Stickley's finishing theory can be found in his own words.

Stickley's Notes on Finishing

... it should be understood that our methods of finishing are for the purpose of getting the best possible results from the wood itself as well as the most pleasing effect in completing the color scheme of a room, and never for the purpose of imitating a more costly wood in the finish of a cheaper one. The beauty of each wood is peculiarly its own, and the sole aim of our finishing is to show that beauty to the best advantage.

That a clearer understanding may be given of the effects we try to obtain with the finishes to be described later, it seems best first to explain the method in ordinary use of furniture and other woodworking establishments, where naturally the effort is made to get the most showy and commercially finished results from the least possible expenditure of time and material. In such cases the wood is first "filled" with prepared wood filler made from a very finely ground silex. When this preparation is carefully rubbed into the pores, the surface of the wood becomes as smooth and even as glass. After the filler has become thoroughly dry, the wood is varnished and rubbed, and either polished to a mirror-like brilliancy or left "in the dull." This destroys the texture by covering it with an enamel that completely alters its character. Whether dull or polished, the woodiness of texture that is so interesting has given place to an artificial smoothness of surface that passes for fineness of finish and that makes all wood alike to the touch.

It is easy to finish wood in this way and yet leave it natural in color, if desired, for the filler made from silex is colorless. If a darker or different color is required, the pigment is usually mixed with the filler. This gives a finish in which the figure of the wood is made very prominent, for the reason that, when the color is carried on in that way, the pigment does not penetrate the glassy surface of the pith ray or figure, and is rubbed off by the same operation that rubs it into the softer parts of the wood. This effect is much sought after in showy furniture, where a highly emphasized figure is considered very desirable, but it is just what we seek most earnestly to avoid, as the figure in the woods mentioned above is already so strong that it needs to be subdued by an even tone rather than heightened by a marked contrast.

Of the woods in the class we are discussing now, oak and chestnut are the only ones affected by the fumes of ammonia. As was discovered some years ago by the use of oaken beams and panelling in the woodwork of fine stables, the effect of ammonia on this wood is to produce quickly the mellow darkness of hue that formerly was supposed to come from age alone. Careful experiment showed that this effect resulted from a certain affinity between the tannic acid in the wood and the ammonia with which the air was heavily charged, and that the same result could be artificially produced by subjecting to the fumes of strong ammonia any wood which contained a sufficient percentage of tannin. This process is the only one known that acts upon the glassy pith rays as well as the softer parts of the wood, coloring all together in an even tone so that the figure is marked only by its difference in texture. This result can not be accomplished by stains, and for this reason we always subject these woods to more or less fuming before applying a stain.

In fuming woods the best results are obtained by shutting the piece into an air-tight box or closet, on the floor of which has been placed a shallow dish containing liquor ammonia (26 per cent). The length of time required to fume to a good color depends largely upon the tightness of the compartment, but as a rule forty-eight hours is enough. Where fuming is not practicable, as in the case of a piece too large for any available compartment, or of the trim of a room, a satisfactory result can be obtained by applying liquor ammonia (26 per cent) directly to the wood with a sponge or brush. In either case, the wood must be in its natural condition when treated, as any previous application of oil or stain would prevent the ammonia from taking effect.

After the wood is thoroughly dry from the first application, sandpaper it carefully with fine sandpaper, then apply another coat of ammonia and sandpaper as before.

Some pieces fume much darker than others, according to the amount of tannin left free to attract the ammonia after the wood has been kiln-dried. Where any sapwood had been left on, that part will be found unaffected by the fumes. To meet these conditions, it is necessary to make a "touch-up" to even up the color. This is done by mixing Vandyke brown, ground in Japan, with German lacquer [clear lacquer], commonly known as "banana liquid," and adding a very little lampblack, also ground in Japan. The mixture may be thinned with wood alcohol to the right consistency for use, and the color of the piece to be touched up will decide the proportion of black to be added to the brown. In touching up the lighter portions of the wood, the stain may be smoothly blended with the dark tint of the perfectly fumed parts by rubbing along the line where they join with a piece of soft, dry cheesecloth, closely following the brush. If the stain should dry too fast and the color is left uneven, dampen the cloth slightly with alcohol.

After fuming, sandpapering and touching up a piece of furniture, apply a coat of lacquer made of one-third white shellac and two-thirds German lacquer. If the fuming process has resulted in a shade dark enough to be satisfactory, this lacquer may be applied clear, if not, it may be darkened by the addititon of a small quantity of the stain used in touching up. Care must be taken, however, not to add enough color to show laps and brushmarks. The danger of this makes it often more advisable to apply two coats of lacquer, each containing a very little color. If this is done, sandpaper each coat with very fine sandpaper after it is thoroughly dry, and then apply one or more coats of prepared floor wax. These directions, if carefully followed, should give the same effects that characterize the Craftsman furniture.

Sometimes it is not deemed practicable or desirable to fume oak or chestnut. In such a case a finish may be used for which directions will be given, and which applies to all woods in this class. For these woods a water stain should never be used, as it raises the grain to such an extent that in sandpapering to make it smooth again the color is sanded off with the grain, leaving an unevenly stained and very unpleasant surface. The most satisfactory method we know, especially for workers who have had but little experience, is to use quick-drying colors (colors ground in Japan) mixed with German lacquer. Both can be obtained at almost any paint shop. After getting the desired shade of the color chosen, apply as quickly as possible, as it dries very rapidly. It is best to cover a small portion of the surface at a time, and then go over it with a soft, dry cloth, to "even it up" before it dries. When it is ready for the final finish, apply a coat of white shellac, sandpaper carefully and apply one or more coats of wax.

Fuming Tent

We have based our fuming tent on those used at the Craftsman workshops. Instead of tarred canvas, however, we substituted heavy (4 mil), clear plastic stapled to a collapsible pine frame. The tent frame is built of five panels, each panel reinforced at the corners with a nailed and glued plywood triangular corner plate (figure 4-41).

The panels are assembled to form the tent by using carriage bolts and wing nuts through holes drilled at the corners of the frame. When ready to fume, assemble three sides and the top of the tent, leaving one end open for access. The final panel is secured into place after the furniture and ammonia have been placed inside the tent.

4-41. Fuming tent, showing plywood corner braces and plastic walls.

Testing for Color

It is advisable to run a test with small scraps of wood from the furniture, since pieces of wood may darken at different rates when exposed to the ammonia fumes. A test will give you some idea of what to expect when you put your furniture into the tent for full-scale fuming. In order for the test to be most helpful, you should make notes of relative times and color changes for each sample.

To conduct a test, you will need a cardboard box large enough to hold the scraps of wood you are testing, a large plastic trash bag (big enough so the box can be placed inside and the bag securely fastened around it), a small glass container, and a small amount of 26 percent aqua ammonia, available from chemical or blueprint supply houses.

First, cut each scrap in half and mark both halves with the same letter. Place the cardboard box inside the plastic bag, and place one-half of each scrap into the box so that no two pieces are touching. The remaining halves should be set aside for comparison with the fumed pieces.

Important: Every precaution must be taken when working with the ammonia during the test and the actual fuming! The fumes are extremely dangerous and harmful if inhaled or in contact with skin. Always work outside. Hold open containers away from you when handling and avoid breathing the fumes or getting the solution on your skin. Read and follow manufacturer's instructions carefully at all times.

Pour ¼ cup (.06 l) of ammonia into the glass container, and place

it into the box with the wood pieces. Close the box and secure the bag around it with a tie.

Check the samples after two hours for color change. Again, open the bag and box carefully because of the accumulated fumes. Remove the fumed scraps and compare them to their matching halves. Note the degree of color change that has taken place (figure 4-42). If a deeper tone is desired, return the pieces to the box and continue fuming. Check the samples every two to three hours until the desired color is reached. When testing is complete, return any remaining ammonia to its container *immediately.*

The length of fuming time will probably vary for each sample piece. Color choice is a matter of personal taste; however, care should be taken not to overfume,

thereby changing the character of the oak by making it unnaturally dark.

The results of this test will help you determine what to look for as you fume your finished furniture in the tent. The length of time required for desired color is not necessarily predictable, since the concentration of fumes in the box may be greater than in the larger tent. By matching the samples to the furniture parts from which they came, however, you will be able to determine which pieces or areas will take a longer or shorter fuming time. Note the location of any wood which has darkened especially fast. Be sure to check that part of the piece of furniture when assessing progress in the tent. Other areas of the furniture can be darkened slightly with stain to even out the color, but if one

area of the furniture piece reacts more quickly than other areas, it will be too dark when the rest of the piece has reached its optimum color.

Fuming

When you load the tent, allow space around each piece for the fumes to act on all surfaces. Parts that must come in contact with another surface should be elevated from that surface with small wooden blocks to allow fumes to circulate underneath. Place several shallow dishes on the floor of the tent (figure 4-43). Starting from the rear of the tent, pour ammonia into each dish; back your way out of the tent, filling the dishes as you go. Work as quickly as possible. Close the end of the tent and fasten in place with wing nuts.

Because the tent sides are made of clear plastic, you can check the progress of the fuming without opening the tent. When the desired color is reached, carefully remove the end panel and allow the tent to air out. Cut some cardboard squares large enough to cover the ammonia dishes. When some of the fumes have dissipated, quickly cover the dishes with the cardboard, leave the tent, and allow time for the remaining fumes to dissipate. Remove the dishes, keeping the covers intact, and pour any remaining ammonia back into the original container. You can then safely remove the furniture pieces from the tent.

With fuming complete, you may continue with the finishing process as described by Stickley above. This will give you the exact method by which his Craftsman furniture was finished and results in a warm, even, rich finish that will withstand the test of time.

4-42. Both blocks in each pair are from the same board. The left blocks are unfumed; those on the right were fumed for eight hours.

Alternate Finishing Method

The following alternate method is offered for those who wish a simpler procedure than the one given by Stickley. Its results are quite satisfactory.

To touch up areas after fuming that are either uneven in color or contain unfumed sapwood, use a mixture of clear penetrating resin oil and enough oil stain of an appropriate tint or mixture of tints to even the surface color. Use the fumed test samples to match colors. When you have achieved the proper color, apply it locally to the desired areas with a brush and allow it to penetrate for approximately fifteen to twenty minutes. Wipe off the excess with a clean cotton cloth and allow to dry for approximately twenty-four hours. This touch-up process may not be necessary. If not, you may proceed as follows after fuming.

A mixture of one part penetrating resin oil and one part clear satin-finish polyurethane varnish, with tint added if desired, forms the final finish. Mixing should be done in a clean metal can. Heat the finish on an electric hot plate set at medium (do *not* use open flame). This heating provides greater penetration of the finish into the wood. Brush the finish over the surface, making sure to soak the entire piece generously. Allow the finish to penetrate for a few minutes, then apply more to any dull areas. Continue this procedure until the entire surface remains wet for about forty-five minutes. Using clean cotton rags, wipe the surface *with the grain*, removing any surface finish which has not penetrated. Allow the piece to dry for twenty-four hours, checking intermittently and wiping dry any spots of finish that bleed from the wood. This bleeding indicates maximum penetration of the finish.

Repeat this procedure two or three more times, allowing the furniture to sit for at least twenty-four hours between each application. This process will give you a finish comparable to Stickley's original method.

HARDWARE

Some of the projects in this book require metal hardware such as hinges, door-pulls, and table irons. Hinges and table irons can be purchased, but door-pulls like Stickley's must be made. A drawing of the door-pulls for the book case is provided in the project section. Having these pulls made (or making them yourself) will give the finished piece an authenticity and integrity well worth the effort or expense.

To Stickely hardware was just as important to each piece of furniture as its design, wood selection, and finishing.

We found out very soon after we began to make the plain oak furniture that even

4-43. Elevate pieces to be fumed and space shallow dishes on the floor of the tent.

the best of the usual machine-made and highly polished metal trim was absurdly out of place, and that in order to get the right thing it was necessary to establish a metal-work department in the Craftsman Workshops where articles of wrought metal in plain rugged designs and possessing the same structural and simple quality as the furniture could be made.

Solid brass or bronze hinges are recommended for those projects requiring them. Solid copper hinges are too soft and are not easily obtainable. Stickley used either brass or copper-plated steel. We suggest that you copper-plate brass or steel hinges in keeping with his procedures. This should be done by a local plating shop. Newly plated hinges are too bright for the character of the furniture and will need further surface treatment.

To give the copper the deep mellow brownish glow that brings it into such perfect harmony with the fumed oak, the finished piece should be rubbed thoroughly with a soft cloth dipped in powdered pumice stone, and then left to age naturally. If a darker tone is desired, it should be held over a fire or torch and heated until the right color appears. Care should be taken that it is not heated too long, as copper under too great heat is apt to turn black. We use no lacquer on either copper or brass, age and exposure being the only agents required to produce beauty and variety of tone. All our brass work is made of the natural unfinished metal, which has a beautiful greenish tone and a soft dull surface that harmonizes admirably with the natural wood. Like copper, it darkens and mellows with age.

The authentic treatment of hardware will add immeasurably to the aesthetic quality of these projects, and knowing the time and care given to each detail by Stickley himself, we feel it is essential to follow his recommendations as completely as possible.

All hardware is put on after finishing is completed. Hinges should be mortised flush to all edges. To do this, measure and mark the position of the hinges on the edges where they will be mounted. Trace around the hinge leaf, using it as a pattern for the mortise. Score the hinge outline with a chisel inside the pencil mark. Cut the mortise to a depth equal to the thickness of the hinge leaf with a flat chisel, working first the length of the mortise and then across it with feathered cuts.

Place the hinge in the mortise and trace around the screw holes with a pencil. Make a punch mark in the center of each circle with a center punch and then drill a pilot hole, using a bit approximately half the diameter of the screw, to a depth equal to that of the screw. The pilot hole must be enlarged to accommodate the shank of the screw to avoid splitting the wood or breaking the screw when it is driven in. Use a drill bit the same diameter as the screw shank and drill into the pilot hole to a depth equal to the length of the shank. When all holes have been prepared, screw the hinge into place.

SEAT FRAMES AND UPHOLSTERY

The following description of seat frame and upholstery construction is taken from an article written by Stickley in *The Craftsman*. This article pertains to a recliner, but the same procedures can be followed for the settle with heavier frame pieces and the number of springs increased proportionately. It offers authentic information invaluable to those who want to construct their seat to his specifications.

. . . the inner seat frame for this chair is made with what is called a slip seat, or a seat that is made and upholstered separately and then slipped inside of the frame of the chair. The seat frame may be made of 1½ inch x ¼ inch hardwood, with the corners mortised and firmly glued. Care should be taken to make it small enough to allow it to slip into the frame of the chair after the leather has been drawn over it, but it should fit tightly into the chair when it is finished.

The seat itself is made by tacking a strip of strong webbing, about 3½ inches wide, over the top of this inner frame. These strips are interlaced like basket work so closely that it is almost solid, and when stretched tightly over the frame and tacked firmly to the wood it forms a strong support. Then twelve springs are sewed to the webbing, care being taken to place them where the strands cross and to stitch them firmly, so that the support afforded will be as strong as possible. Then a strong cord is stretched over the tops of the springs to hold them in place. This should be drawn down tightly both ways and tied to each spring as it passes over it, making all firm and secure so that no amount of wear will make the springs slip out of place. It is important that care should be exercised in this matter, as it would be very difficult to adjust a spring after the leather is on. After the springs are securely fastened to the webbing a layer of burlap should be stretched over them and tacked to the edge of the frame. This also should be drawn very tightly and sewed to each spring. Then a layer of tow, about 1 inch in depth should be laid evenly over the burlap and sewn firmly down to it. Upon the top of this some loose tow should be spread, taking care to leave no lumps or hollows, and this again should be covered with a smoothly-packed layer of curled hair about 2 inches in depth, special care being taken to build up the edges firmly and evenly. Another layer of burlap is then placed over the hair, and the edges are stitched so that the hair is kept in place and the edges well filled. Lastly the leather is stretched over the frame and tacked to it as already described. The seat is now ready to slip into the frame of the chair, where it is held firmly by two cleats screwed to the front and back rails to afford support for the inner seat frame. The back itself is not upholstered, but is made comfortable by a large, loose cushion covered with soft leather or sheepskin and filled with cotton floss.

5. Projects

The instinct of doing things is a common one, and can be made a source of pleasure, healthy discipline and usefulness, even when the work is taken up as a recreation, and it is this purpose mainly that this series of Home Training in Cabinet-Work is intended to serve.

When one has made with his own hands any object of use or ornament there is a sense of personal pride and satisfaction in the result, that no expenditure of money can buy, and this very fact serves to dignify the task and to stamp it with individuality.

This quote comes from a series of articles entitled "Home Training in Cabinet Work: Practical Talks on Structural Woodworking," written by Stickley and first appearing in the March, 1905, issue of *The Craftsman*.

We have chosen nine pieces of furniture designed by Stickley as projects for this book. Five pieces: the screen, combination bookcase and table, recliner, bookcase, and clock case, come from the Home Training in Cabinet-Work series; four projects: the mirror, rocker, settle, and dining table, are based upon pieces produced at the Eastwood factory.

Our selections were based upon the fundamental furnishing needs of most homes. We were also concerned about project complexity and have provided projects requiring varying skill levels. Specific information about each project such as measurements and special joinery are found under the title for that project. General construction information pertaining to all (or at least several) projects is given in chapter 4 and will be referenced as needed.

The materials list for each project contains only those items specific to that project. General woodworking tools and materials, described in chapter 4, are not included on these lists, although they will be needed to complete the projects.

All measurements not given in the project instructions can be found in the working drawings that accompany each project.

Mirror

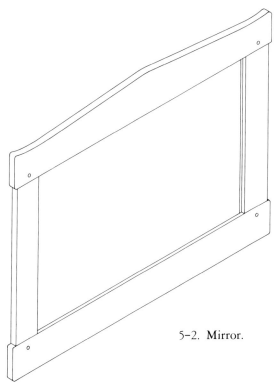

5–2. Mirror.

A mirror is a simple but very functional piece of furniture that can enhance any room. The graceful curve of this Craftsman design, with its slight lift at the ends, and the extension of both horizontal members past their vertical intersections soften an otherwise harsh rectangular shape. Instead of a sharply punctuated hole, this mirror forms a soft silhouette.

The mirror is an easy piece to construct, consisting of five pieces. Four pieces comprise the frame; the fifth piece is the back panel, which holds the mirror in place. Cut your stock to the dimensions given in the materials list. The top of the mirror is cut on a band saw using a pattern made from dimensions given in figure 5-3.

in.	cm
⅜	.95
¾	1.91
3	7.62
4	10.16
4¾	12.08
19	48.26
27¾	70.50
36	91.44

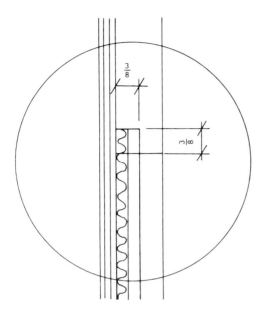

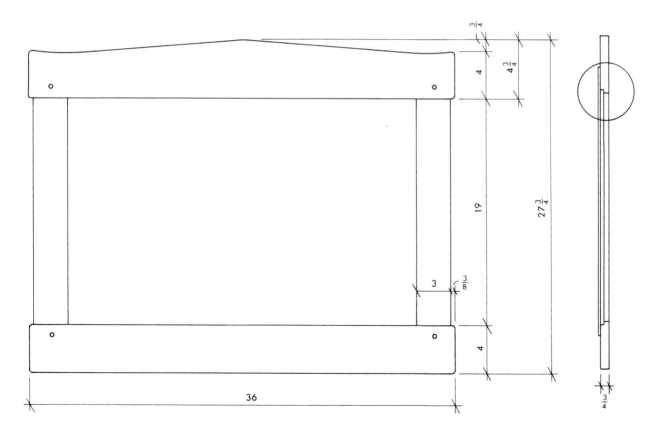

5-3. Working drawings for mirror. Front view, side view, cross section, and cross section detail.

MATERIALS

	Number of Pieces	Length		Width		Thickness	
		in.	cm	in.	cm	in.	cm
Top	1	36	91.44	4¾	12.06	¾	1.91
				(pattern-cut)			
Bottom	1	36	91.44	4	10.16	¾	1.91
Side	2	21½	54.61	3	7.62	¾	1.91
Back Panel	1	33	83.82	23	58.42	⅜	.95

⅜-inch (.95-cm) dowels
1 piece cardboard, 29¼ × 19¾ × ¼ (74.30 × 50.17 × .64 cm)
1 mirror, 29¼ × 19¾ × ⅛ inches (74.30 × 50.17 × .32 cm)
14 brass flathead wood screws

PROCEDURE

In addition to the instructions given below, you may need to refer to the general instructions in chapter 4 for the following procedures:

Cutting tenons, pages 65–66
Cutting mortises with drill and chisel, page 69
Dowel-pinning, pages 82–83
Assembly, pages 79–83
Finishing, pages 84–87

Frame
Join the frame at the corners with blind mortise-and-tenon joints. Cut the tenons on the vertical members to fit into mortises cut into the horizontal members. Each tenon is 2 inches (5.08 cm) wide by 1¼ inches (3.17 cm) long by ⅜-inches (.95 cm) thick.

After assembling the frame, pin the tenons in place with ⅜ inch (.95 cm) dowels. Locate the center of each dowel ¾ inch (1.91 cm) from the seam line, centered on the tenon.

Assembly
Following subassembly of the frame, cut a ⅜-inch-deep (.95-cm) rabbet into the back side of the frame with a 1⅜-inch (.95-cm) rabbeting bit (see circle detail drawing, figure 5-3).

Apply a finish to the piece, using the procedure described in chapter 4.

Insert the mirror, with the cardboard behind it, into the rabbet that was cut into the frame. The cardboard prevents the silvering from being scratched off the back of the mirror. The mirror and cardboard are held in place by the back panel, a piece of oak plywood. Attach this panel to the back of the frame with brass flathead wood screws. Sand the edges and corners of the plywood backing until they are soft.

Screen

A folding screen is a very versatile item. It can be used to shade an area from light, divide a large room into smaller spaces, accent a corner, or provide privacy. The screen shown here is made in three sections. The lower part of each section has panels connected with butterfly joints, and the upper area of each section is covered with a curtain held in place by a brass rod.

93

5-5. Exploded view of screen; butterfly joints not shown.

MATERIALS

	Number of Pieces	Length		Width		Thickness	
		in.	cm	in.	cm	in.	cm
Frame							
Sides	6	60	152.40	2¼	5.71	⅞	2.22
Top Rail	3	17½	44.45	4¼	10.80	⅞	2.22
				(pattern-cut)			
Center Rail	3	17½	44.45	2¼	5.71	⅞	2.22
Bottom Rail	3	17½	44.45	4	10.16	⅞	2.22
Panels							
Outer Panel	6	16	40.64	5	12.70	½	1.27
Center Panel	3	16	40.64	6½	16.51	½	1.27
Spline	6	16	40.64	1½	3.81	⅛	.32
Butterfly Joints							
Butterfly	12	2¾	6.98	1⁹⁄₁₆	3.97	⅝	1.58
				(pattern-cut)			

⅜-inch (.95-cm) dowels
6 brass rods, ¼-inch (.64-cm) diameter, 16½ inches (41.91 cm) long
4 1¾-inch (4.44 cm) double-acting brass or steel hinges
3¼ yards (2.97 m) curtain fabric

Each section of the screen is made from ten pieces plus butterfly joints. Five pieces (two sides and three rails) make up each frame, and five pieces (two outer panels, one center panel, and two splines), plus butterflies, comprise the paneling. Cut your stock to the dimensions given in the materials list. The curved top of each section is cut on a band saw following a pattern made according to the dimensions given in figure 5-8 (see figure 5-6).

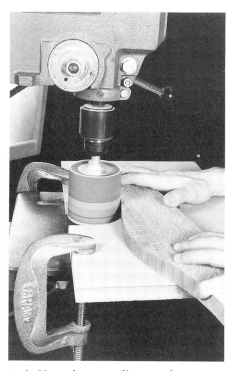

5-6. Use a drum sanding attachment on a drill press to sand the pattern cut in the top rails.

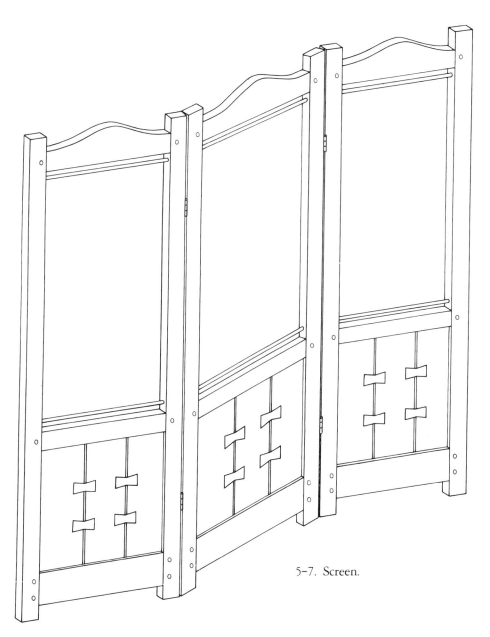

5-7. Screen.

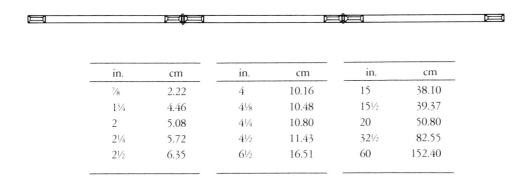

in.	cm	in.	cm	in.	cm
7/8	2.22	4	10.16	15	38.10
1¾	4.46	4⅛	10.48	15½	39.37
2	5.08	4¼	10.80	20	50.80
2¼	5.72	4½	11.43	32½	82.55
2½	6.35	6½	16.51	60	152.40

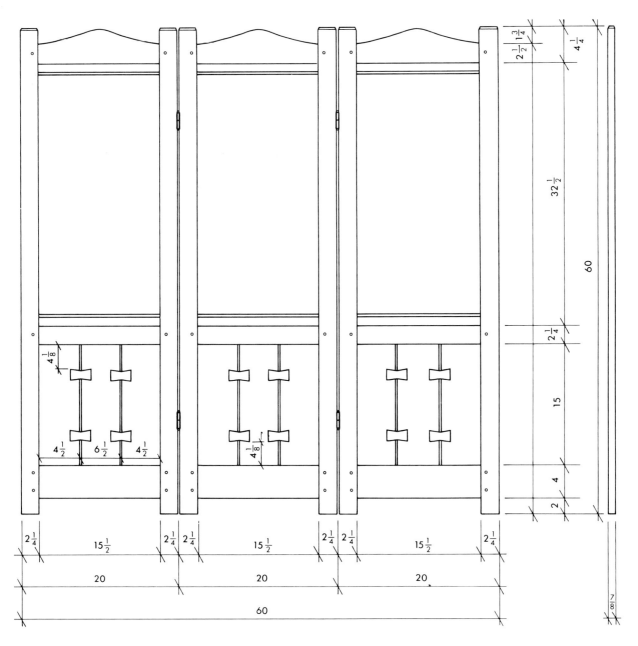

5-8. Working drawings for screen. Top, front, and side views.

PROCEDURE

In addition to the instructions given below, you may need to refer to the general instructions in chapter 4 for the following procedures:

Cutting tenons, pages 65–66
Cutting mortises with router table, pages 76–77
Dowel-pinning, pages 82–83
Beveling, page 70
Attaching hinges, page 88
Assembly, pages 79–83
Finishing, pages 84–87

Frame

Join the frame with blind mortise-and-tenon joints. The tenons on the top and center rails are 1½ inches (3.81 cm) wide by 1 inch (2.54 cm) long by ½ inch (1.27 cm) thick. Use a router table to cut the mortises in the side.

Cut a ½-inch-deep (1.27-cm) dado in the top of the bottom rail, the bottom of the center rail, and the sides, on center, with a ½ inch (1.27-cm) dado blade (figures 5-9 and 5-10). These will accommodate the panels.

Using a ¼-inch (.64-cm) bit, drill holes for the curtain rods on the inside edges of each side of the frames. Locate these holes 1 inch (2.54 cm), on center, below the mortises for the top rails to hold the top rods and above the mortises for the center rails to hold the bottom rods. Drill the two holes on the left side of each frame 1 inch (2.54 cm) deep and the two holes on the right side of each frame ½ inch (1.27 cm) deep. The extra depth on the left sides allows for easy insertion and removal of the brass rods when installing the curtains.

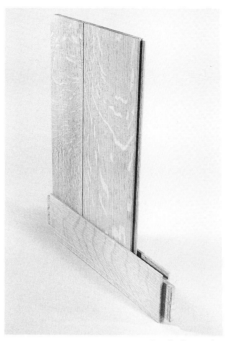

5-9. Two panels resting in the dado cut in the bottom rail.

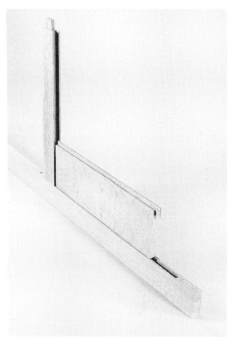

5-10. One panel resting in dado cut in the side and the center rails. Note spline in edge of panel.

5-11. Cutting the spline dado in the edge of a panel.

Panels

Make cuts ¾ inch (1.91 cm) deep and ⅛ inch (.32 cm) wide, on center, into the panels' edges to accommodate the splines (figure 5-11). Using the router table and a beading bit, slightly bevel the splined edge of each face of all panels, as shown in figure 5-12.

Round the two outside corners of each outer panel as shown, to allow for movement and ease in assembly.

Subassembly

Assemble each frame by applying glue to only the mortise-and-tenon joints (figure 5-13); allow the whole panel section free movement. This movement is necessary to prevent the panels from splitting or putting undue pressure on the frame if they expand.

Pin each tenon in place with a ⅜-inch (.95-cm) dowel that penetrates the full thickness of the frame and shows on both sides. Use one dowel on each of the tenons for the top and center rails. Locate the center of each dowel ½ inch (1.27 cm) from the seam line, centered on the tenon. Pin the bottom rail in place with two dowels on each end. Place the dowels' centers ½ inch (1.27 cm)

from the seam line and 2 inches (5.08 cm) apart, on center.

Bevel the top of each side of the sections with a block and sandpaper. Cut the bevel using guidelines placed ⅛ inch (.32 cm) down from the top edge on each side and ⅛ inch (.32 cm) in from all edges.

Butterfly Joints

The butterfly joints are the last pieces to be made and fitted. They prevent the loose panels from separating along their seams and add a decorative motif to the panels.

To prepare the panels, make a cardboard template of the butterfly, using the dimensions given

5-12. Beveling the splined edge of a panel on the router table with a beading bit.

5-13. Frame clamped with bar clamps. Check the frame for alignment using a combination or framing square.

in figure 5-14. With this template, draw the location of each butterfly on the panels. Drill ½-inch (1.27-cm) holes in each of the butterfly "wings." Draw guidelines from each hole to the corners of the wing, as shown in figure 5-15. With a keyhole saw, cut along the guidelines. To finish each butterfly hole, remove the last piece of material with a flat chisel, bevel facing in (figure 5-16).

Using the same template, draw outlines of the butterflies on ⅝-inch-thick (1.58-cm) stock, making sure the template is placed so that its length is parallel to the grain of the wood. Cut the butterflies slightly oversize and file each to fit its hole. Then mark each butterfly and its hole with the same letter or number. When all butterflies are fitted, glue each in place, allowing a ¹⁄₁₆-inch (.15-cm) projection from the panel faces on both sides.

Final Touches

Apply a finish to the piece, using the procedure described in chapter 4.

Because of the special movements required by a folding screen, double-acting hinges should be used. Two hinges join each section pair, one placed 10½ inches (26.67 cm) down from the top and the other 10½ inches (26.67 cm) up from the bottom.

Curtains for the screen should be made of plain, neutral-colored fabric of medium weight, such as linen. Each fabric panel is gathered on the solid brass rods at top and bottom.

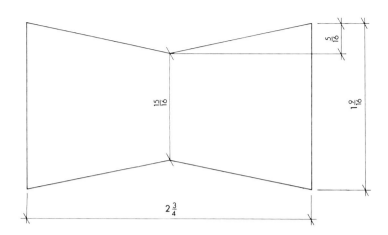

5-14. Working drawing for butterfly.

in.	cm
⁵⁄₁₆	.79
¹⁵⁄₁₆	2.38
1⁹⁄₁₆	3.96
2¼	6.98

5-15. Cutting butterfly joint with a keyhole saw.

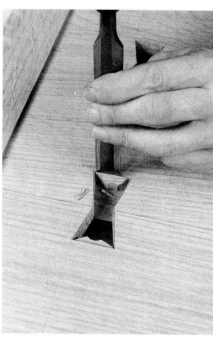

5-16. Removing remaining material with a flat chisel, bevel of chisel facing in.

Combination Bookcase and Table

This piece of furniture was originally designed by Stickley for students who found it necessary to have their books as close at hand as their writing pad. The table surface is high enough to be used as a writing surface when the user is seated on most side chairs. The shelf area is divided into quarters to take advantage of the full shelf as storage space; books can be stored on all four sides. This Craftsman piece is designed to bear heavy loads.

The combination bookcase and table is composed of fifty-four pieces. Twelve pieces: four legs, four top rails, and four bottom rails, comprise the frame. The bottom shelf, composed of several boards laminated edge-to-edge, contains thirty-six slats, which form the book holders. Four cleats support the tabletop, which is also made from several boards laminated edge-to-edge. Cut your stock to the dimensions given in the materials list.

5-18. Exploded view of combination bookcase and table.

5-19. Combination bookcase and table.

MATERIALS

	Number of Pieces	Length in.	Length cm	Width in.	Width cm	Thickness in.	Thickness cm
Frame							
Leg	4	31	78.74	1¾	4.44	1¾	4.44
Rail	8	23	58.42	2	5.08	⅞	2.22
Bottom Shelf and Slats							
Shelf	1	21¾	55.26	21¾	55.26	¾	1.91
Slat	36	15¼	38.74	1	2.54	½	1.27
Cleats							
Cleat	4	23¼	59.06	1	2.54	⅝	1.58
Tabletop							
Top	1	28	71.12	28	71.12	⅞	2.22

⅜-inch (.95-cm) dowels
8 table irons
16 steel flathead wood screws

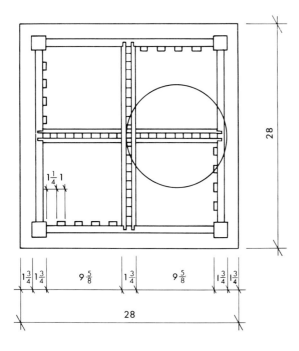

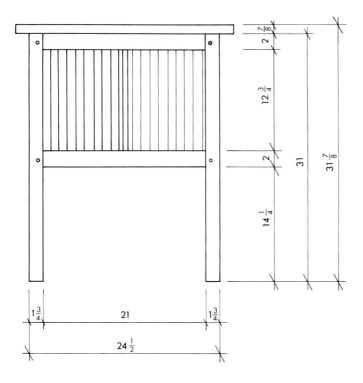

PROCEDURE

In addition to the instructions given below, you may need to refer to the general instructions in chapter 4 for the following procedures:

Cutting tenons, pages 65–66
Cutting mortises with router table, pages 76–77
Butt-joining, page 71
Cutting mortises with drill and chisel, page 69
Dowel-pining, pages 82–83
Squaring laminated boards, pages 74–75
Assembly, pages 79–83
Finishing, pages 84–87

Frame

The mortise-and-tenon joint is the main joint used for the construction of this piece. Connect the rails and legs with blind mortise-and-tenon joints (figure 5-21).

in.	cm
⅞	2.22
1	2.54
1¼	3.17
1¾	4.44
2	5.08
9⅝	24.44
12¾	32.38
14¼	36.19
21	53.34
24½	62.23
28	71.12
31	78.74
31⅞	80.96

5-20. Working drawings for combination bookcase and table. Top and side view. (For circled detail, see figure 5-25.)

The rail tenons measure 1 inch (2.54 cm) wide by 1 inch (2.54 cm) long by ½ inch (1.27 cm) thick. Measure in $^{11}/_{16}$ inch (1.75 cm) from the two outside faces of each leg to locate the center line for each mortise. Locate the center of each mortise for the bottom rails 15½ inches (39.37 cm) up from the bottom of each leg; those for the top rails, 1 inch (2.54 cm) down from the top of each leg. Cut the mortises with the router table.

Dado the four bottom rails along their inside faces to hold the edge of the shelf. Cut these dados ⅛ inch (.32 cm) down from the top edge, ¾ inch (1.91 cm) wide, to a depth of ⅜ inch (.95 cm) (figure 5-22).

5-21. Blind mortise-and-tenon joints connect top rails with legs.

5-22. Dados cut in bottom rails hold shelf edges.

Bottom Shelf and Slats

Laminate three or four boards (depending on width) edge-to-edge with ⅜-inch (.95-cm) dowels to form the 21¾- by 21¾-inch (55.25- by 55.25-cm) bottom shelf. Notch a ⅜-inch (.95-cm) square on each corner to accommodate the legs.

Cut tenons onto only the bottom ends of the slats. These tenons measure ½ inch (1.27 cm) wide by ⅜ inch (.95 cm) long by ¼ inch (.64 cm) thick. Locate the position of each slat on the shelf (see figures 5-20 and 5-24) and mark the shelf for cutting the mortises. Using a fence or guide clamped to the shelf, cut the mortises with a router and a ¼-inch (.64-cm) straight bit (figure 5-23).

5-24. Insert slats into their mortises and check for proper fit.

5-23. Cut mortises for slats into shelf with a router and fence.

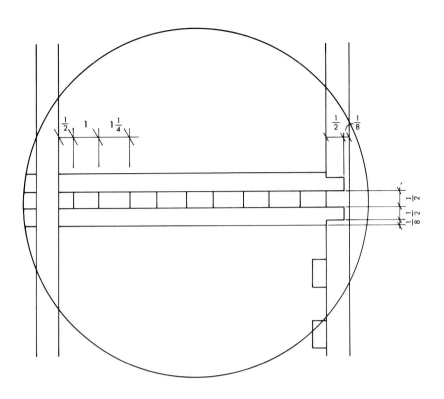

in.	cm
⅛	.32
½	1.27
1	2.54
1¼	3.17

5-25. Detail of cleat joint and slat position.

Cleats

Cut barefaced tenons measuring ¾ inch (1.91 cm) wide by ½ inch (1.27 cm) long by ½ inch (1.27 cm) thick onto both ends of each cleat. Join the four cleats at their centers using an edge cross-lap joint. To make this joint, set a ⅝-inch-wide (1.58-cm) dado blade on the table saw to a depth of ½ inch (1.27 cm). Locate center lines for lap joint cuts 10 ⁹⁄₁₆ inches (26.83 cm) from the end of each cleat. Cut joints using the miter guide as a support. Remember, one pair of cleats should be cut on the top edge and the other pair on the bottom edge (figure 5-26).

Cut mortises, measuring ½ inch (1.27 cm) wide by ¾ inch (1.91 cm) deep by ½ inch (1.27 cm) long, for the barefaced tenons into the top edge and inside face of each top rail (figure 5-27). Locate these mortises 10 inches (25.40 cm), on center, from the inside edge of each post. Cut mortises using the drill and chisel cleanout method.

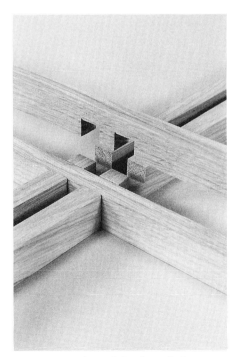

5-26. Four cleats joined at their centers with an edge cross-lap joint.

5-27. Barefaced tenons on cleat ends fit into mortises on inside of top rails.

Subassembly

Assemble frame and bottom shelf as shown in figure 5-28. Pin each rail tenon into the leg with a ⅜-inch (.95-cm) dowel placed ⅝ inch (1.58 cm) from the seam, centered on the tenon. When this assembly is dry, glue the cleats into place and clamp as shown in figure 5-29. Then glue the slats into position, clamping their top ends to the cleats and top rails (figure 5-30).

Tabletop

The tabletop is constructed of three or four pieces of stock (depending on width) laminated edge-to-edge with ⅜-inch (.95-cm) dowels. Lay out the top, being careful to alternate the end grain direction to minimize warping. Using a router, trim one end square, then measure to length and trim the other end.

Final Touches

Apply a finish to the piece, using the procedure described in chapter 4.

The top is held in position on the base with eight table irons. Countersink the irons into the top edge of the top rails above the open area in each side, as shown in figure 5-31. Place the first iron 5 inches (12.70 cm) from the outside corner of each leg and the second iron 9 inches (22.86 cm) from the outside corner of each leg.

5-28. Assembly of frame: legs, rails, and shelf.

5-29. Cleats glued and clamped into top rails.

5-30. Slats assembled and clamped with a C-clamp.

5-31. Table irons in position on top rail.

Rocker

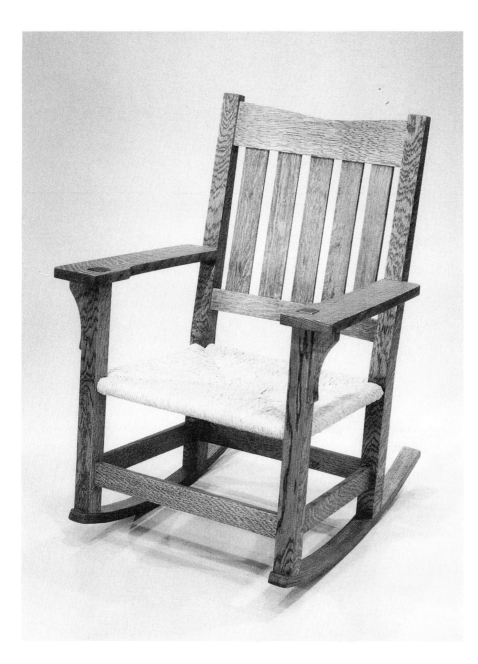

The rocking chair has traditionally been a favorite in American homes. Its rhythmic back-and-forth motion produces a mesmerizing serenity, soothing people of all ages. This Craftsman chair is from a line of rockers produced at Stickley's Eastwood factory.

Of all pieces of furniture, chairs are the most difficult to build because of the critical alignment of their many parts and the large number of surfaces to finish. In the rocking chair, these factors are compounded by bent horizontal back slats and rockers. We recommend that you begin this project by drawing full-size drawings of the side and top cross section views of the chair (see figures 5-35 and 5-36). The side view will give you the correct angle to cut the shoulders of the front and back stretchers.

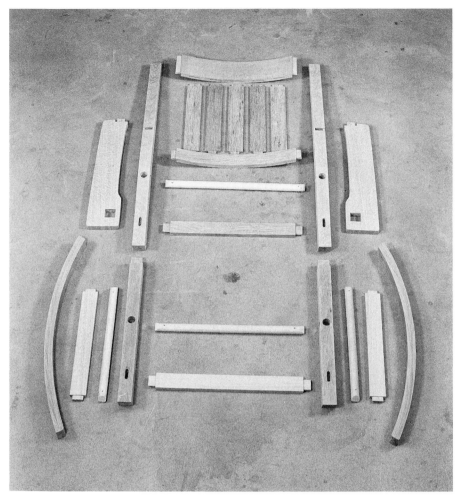

5-33. Exploded view of rocker.

The rocker consists of twenty-five pieces. Its frame has four legs connected near their bottoms by four stretchers, one in front, one in back, and one on each side. Four dowels connected to the legs comprise the seat frame. The back consists of two bent, horizontal slats attached to the back legs. Five vertical slats that provide support are connected to these two horizontal slats. The two arms are supported by arm supports on the front legs. Two bent, laminated boards form each rocker, which is attached on either side to the front and back legs. Cut your stock according to the dimensions given in the materials list. Use paper patterns to accurately cut the front and back legs, top horizontal back slat, arms, and arm supports.

5-34. Rocker.

MATERIALS

	Number of Pieces	Length in.	cm	Width in.	cm	Thickness in.	cm
Frame							
Front Leg	2	21	53.34	1¾	4.44	1¾	4.44
Back Leg	2	33⅝	85.40	(pattern-cut)		1¾	4.44
Front Stretcher	1	20¼	51.44	2	5.08	⅝	1.58
Back Stretcher	1	19	48.26	2	5.08	⅝	1.58
Side Stretcher	2	16¾	42.55	2	5.08	⅝	1.58
Seat Frame							
Front Dowel	1	20¼	51.44			1 (diam.)	2.54
Back Dowel	1	19	48.26			1 (diam.)	2.54
Side Dowel	2	16¾	42.55			1 (diam.)	2.54
Rockers							
Rocker	2	29 / 32 (radius)	73.66 / 81.28	1¾	4.44	1⅛	2.86
Back							
Bottom Horizontal Back Slat	1	19¼ / 23 (radius)	48.90 / 58.42	2	5.08	⅝	1.58
Top Horizontal Back Slat	1	19¼ / 23 (radius)	48.90 / 58.42	4 (pattern-cut)	10.16	⅝	1.58
Vertical Back Slat	5	14¼	36.20	2⁵⁄₁₆	5.87	⅜	.95
Arms							
Arm	2	19¼	48.90	4½ (pattern-cut)	11.43	⅞	2.22
Arm Support	2	5⅞	14.92	1¾ (pattern-cut)	4.44	1	2.54 .

⅜-inch (.95-cm) dowels
¾-inch (1.91-cm) dowels
rush seat

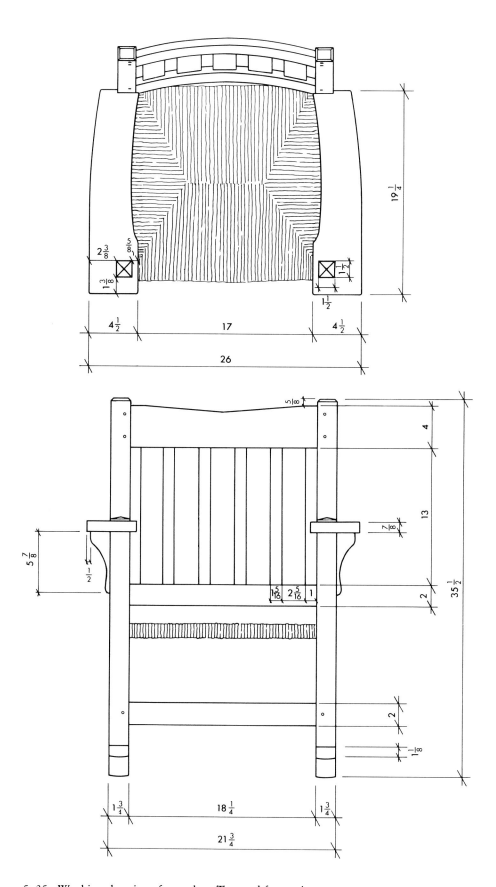

in.	cm
½	1.28
⅝	1.58
⅞	2.22
1	2.54
1⅛	2.86
1⁵⁄₁₆	3.33
1⅜	3.49
1½	3.81
1¾	4.44
2	5.08
2¼	5.71
2⁵⁄₁₆	5.87
2⅜	6.03
4	10.16
4½	11.43
5⅞	14.92
13	33.02
17	43.18
18¼	46.35
19¼	48.89
21¾	55.24
26	66.04
35½	90.17

5-35. Working drawings for rocker. Top and front views.

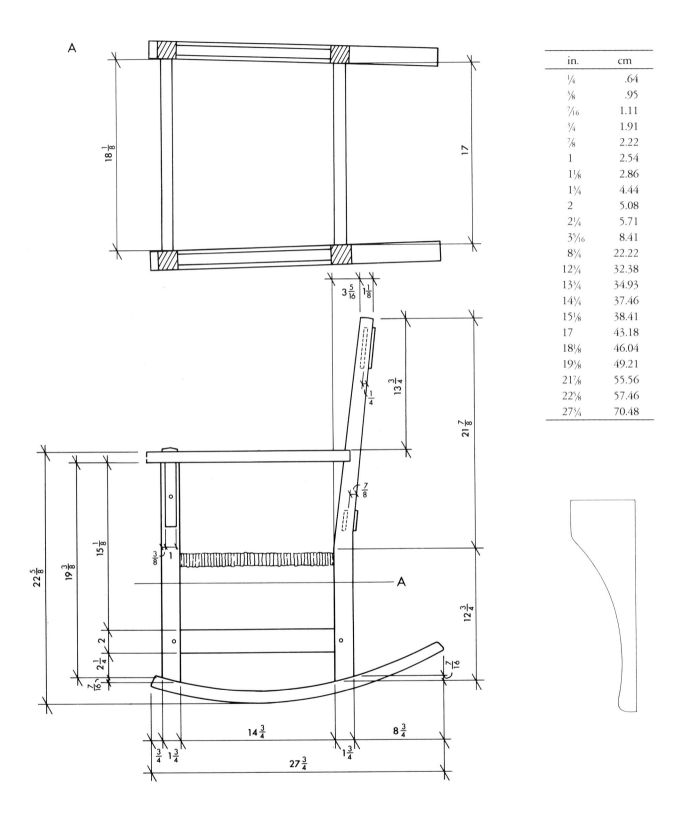

in.	cm
1/4	.64
3/8	.95
7/16	1.11
3/4	1.91
7/8	2.22
1	2.54
1 1/8	2.86
1 3/4	4.44
2	5.08
2 1/4	5.71
3 5/16	8.41
8 3/4	22.22
12 3/4	32.38
13 3/4	34.93
14 3/4	37.46
15 1/8	38.41
17	43.18
18 1/8	46.04
19 5/8	49.21
21 7/8	55.56
22 5/8	57.46
27 3/4	70.48

5-36. Working drawings for rocker. Top view cross section at A, side view, and rocker arm support.

PROCEDURE

In addition to the instructions given below, you may need to refer to the general instructions in chapter 4 for the following procedures:

Cutting tenons, pages 65–66
Cutting mortises with router table, pages 76–77
Bending, pages 77–78
Cutting tenon on bent stock, pages 66–67
Cutting mortises with drill and chisel, page 69
Beveling, page 70
Dowel-pinning, pages 82–83
Assembly, pages 79–83
Finishing, pages 84–87

Frame

Cut blind tenons measuring 1¼ inches (3.17 cm) wide by 1 inch (2.54 cm) long by ⅜ inch (.95 cm) thick on the ends of the four stretchers. Note that the front and back stretchers should have angled shoulders. Locate and cut mortises in the legs to accommodate the stretcher tenons, using the router table.

Seat Frame

The rush seat frame construction requires 1-inch (2.54-cm) diameter birch dowels. Drill 1-inch (2.54-cm) diameter holes into the same faces on the legs, where the stretcher mortises were cut 7⁹/₁₆ inches (19.20 cm) up from the center of each stretcher mortise. Because the holes will meet inside each leg, you must cut the ends of each dowel at a 45-degree angle so they can make full penetration. Mark each dowel and hole for later matching.

Rockers

Bend the rockers and horizontal back slats to the radii given in the

5-37. After rocker halves are bent, apply glue to both pieces.

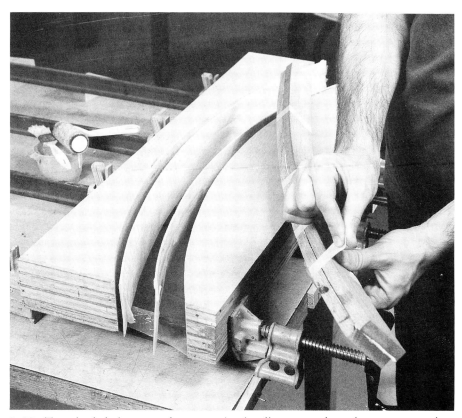

5-38. Tape both halves together to maintain alignment when clamp pressure is applied.

5-39. Rocker halves in mold, with alternating clamps in position.

5-40. With block plane, level one side of each rocker.

5-41. Using a jig to keep rocker from riding up on the blade, trim to width, remembering to put planed side against the fence.

materials list. Because the rockers are so thick, you should construct each from two pieces of stock laminated together.

To laminate a rocker, apply glue to both pieces after the halves are bent (figure 5-37). Tape both halves together to maintain alignment when clamp pressure is applied (figure 5-38). Place the taped halves into the mold and clamp, alternating clamp positions to equalize pressure (figure 5-39). After the glue has dried, remove the rocker from the mold and level one side using a block plane (figure 5-40). Use a table saw, with a jig to keep the rocker from riding up on the blade of the table saw, to level the opposite side. Remember to place the block-planed side against the fence (figure 5-41) when leveling the opposite side with the table saw.

Back

Cut blind tenons measuring $1^{5}/_{16}$ inches (3.33 cm) wide by $\frac{3}{4}$ inch (1.91 cm) long by $\frac{1}{4}$ inch (.64 cm) thick in both ends of the five vertical back slats. Locate mortise positions for these tenons on the two bent horizontal back stats (see figure 5-35 for measurements). Cut these mortises using the drill and chisel cleanout method.

Cut blind tenons onto the ends of both horizontal back slats. The top horizontal tenons measure 3 inches (7.62 cm) wide by 1 inch (2.54 cm) long by $\frac{3}{8}$ inch (.95 cm) thick; the bottom horizontal tenons measure 1 inch (2.54 cm) wide by 1 inch (2.54 cm) long by $\frac{3}{8}$ inch (.95 cm) thick. Cut these bent tenons using the method described in chapter 4. Locate the mortises for these tenons on the legs (see figures 5-35 and 5-36), and cut with the drill and chisel cleanout method.

Cut the curved edge on the top horizontal back slat. At its narrowest point (in the middle of the slat), the slat should be 2¼ inches (5.72 cm) wide.

Arms

Cut each arm with a band saw, using a pattern made from the drawings (figure 5-42). Connect the arm to the front leg with a through mortise-and-tenon joint. Cut through tenons that measure 1½ inches (3.81 cm) wide by 1⅛ inches (2.86 cm) long by 1½ inches (3.81 cm) thick onto the tops of the front legs. Bevel the tenons on the ends, beginning ¹⁵/₁₆ inch (2.38 cm) from the shoulder and meeting in the center to form a peak. Locate the mortises on the arms (see figure 5-35) and cut, using the drill and chisel cleanout method.

Connect the arms to the back leg with blind haunched mortise-and-tenon joints (figure 5-43). Cut a blind haunched tenon in the back of the arm measuring 1 inch (2.54 cm) wide by 1 inch (2.54 cm) long by ½ inch (1.27 cm) thick with a ¼ inch (.64 cm) by ½ inch (1.27 cm) haunch. Begin the tenon cuts ½ inch (1.27 cm) from the inside of each arm, ³/₁₆ inch (.47 cm) down from the top. In order for the shoulders of these tenons to fit flush against the back leg, they must be cut at an angle. The angle can be taken from your full-size side view drawing. Cut these bent tenons using the method described in chapter 4. Locate mortises using the full-size side view drawing, and cut with the drill and chisel cleanout method.

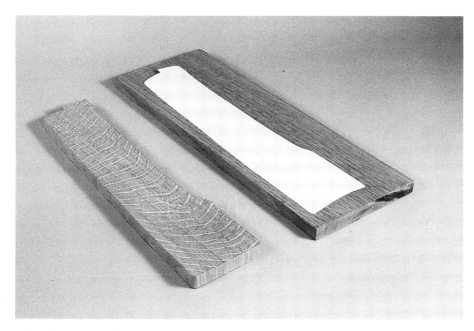

5-42. Place pattern in position and trace onto stock. The same pattern can be used for the other arm. Remember to flip the pattern over before tracing the second arm.

Assembly

Glue together all of the chair's parts except the rockers.

Pin the tenons of the four stretchers with ⅜-inch (.95-cm) dowels placed ⅜ inch (.95 cm) from the inside leg edge, centered on the tenons.

Pin the tenons of the bottom horizontal back slat with a ⅜-inch (.95-cm) dowel placed ⅜ inch (.95 cm) from the inside back leg edge, centered on the tenon. Pin the top horizontal back slat with two ⅜-inch (.95-cm) dowels at each end, placed ⅜ inch (.95 cm) from the inside back leg edge. Locate the top dowel 1¼ inches (3.17 cm) down from the top of the post; center the bottom dowel 2½ inches (6.35 cm) below the top one.

5-43. Shaded area shows material to be removed to make blind haunched tenons.

Pin the through tenon of the front leg to the arm with a ⅜-inch (.95-cm) dowel, centered on the tenon, on the inside edge of the arm.

Cut two arm supports with a band saw, using a pattern made from figure 5-36. Sand each curve, using a drum sanding attachment on a drill press. Glue into place, and pin to the legs with ⅜-inch (.95-cm) dowels placed 2¾ inches (6.98 cm) up from the bottom of the support, on center.

The rockers are now fitted and glued into place. Mark each rocker with a penciled outline of where it meets each leg. Chalk the areas within the lines. Place the rocker in its proper position on the legs and rub back and forth, moving the rocker toward and away from the opposite legs. This will de-

posit chalk on the leg bottoms; those areas on the leg bottoms showing chalk need adjustment. Remove excess stock by filing or block sanding. Repeat until the bottom of each leg is covered with chalk.

To ensure a precise fit, tape #80-grit sandpaper to the curve of the rocker, and trim it to the exact width of the rocker. Draw a series of pencil lines diagonally across the bottom of each leg. Sand by moving the rocker with the same motion described above until the pencil marks are gone. Glue the rockers to the legs, as shown in figure 5-44.

To reinforce this joint, use a 2-inch-long (5.08-cm), ¾-inch (1.91-cm) dowel. Drill a ¾-inch (1.91-cm) diameter hole to a depth of 1⅞ inches (4.76 cm), on center on

each leg, through the rocker. Cut a ¾-inch-deep (1.91-cm) slot into both ends of each dowel; the slots on one end should be perpendicular to those on the other (figure 5-45). Insert ½-inch-long (1.27-cm) wedges into the slots; when the dowel is glued and driven into place, these wedges expand and lock the dowel in position.

Final Touches

With a file or hand plane, remove protruding dowels and slightly round the bottom surface of each rocker. Bevel the top of each back leg with a block and sandpaper. Cut these bevels according to guidelines placed ⅛ inch (.32 cm) down from the top edge on each side and ⅛ inch (.32 cm) in from all edges on the top.

Apply a finish to the piece using the procedure described in chapter 4.

The rush seat should be completed after the chair has been fumed and finished. The rush seat could be woven by the builder with the help of a text on the subject or done by a professional.

5-44. Before clamps are put in position, tape a piece of pine to the top edge of the side stretcher to prevent damage from clamps.

5-45. Dowel in position, with opposing slots. Perpendicular slots prevent the dowel from splitting when driven into place. Wedges are cut ½ inch (1.27 cm) in length to assure full penetration.

Recliner

The mechanics of this chair are based upon a design that has been adapted by many furniture designers. The original mechanical concept is attributed to the British Arts and Crafts designer William Morris, and often these chairs, no matter what they look like, are called Morris chairs.

This recliner is one of several designed by Stickley. It is constructed of heavy members and meant to remain in a more or less fixed position in a room, unlike a rocker or side chair. The back of the recliner is fastened to the inside of the legs with pins, upon which it pivots. The back can be adjusted to four positions: the posts of the back rest on adjusting pins that can be inserted in any of the four pairs of holes drilled in the back inside edges of the arms. The many through mortise-and-tenon joints in this chair demonstrate Stickley's philosophy of structural ornament.

Begin this project by making a full-size drawing of the side view of the recliner (see figure 5-50). This will give you patterns for the angle cuts on the top and bottom side rails, the tops and bottoms of the side slats, the profiles of the arms, and the angles of the shoulders at the tops of the back legs.

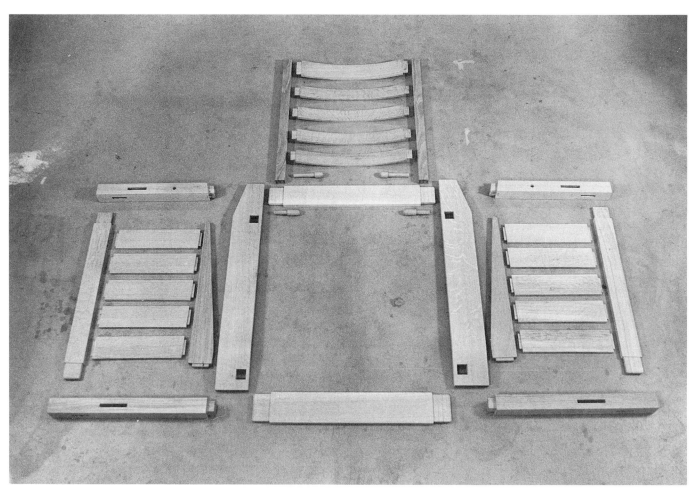

5-47. Exploded view of recliner.

5-48. Recliner.

Three subassemblies are required to build this chair: two sides, each assembled independently, and the back. Each side is made up of twelve pieces: two legs, two rails, five slats, one arm, and two arm supports. The back consists of seven pieces: two posts, a top horizontal slat, and four bottom horizontal slats. Once the sides are assembled, they are connected by a front and back rail, forming the base of the chair. The back is then attached with four removable pins. Cut your stock according to the dimensions given in the materials list.

MATERIALS

	Number of Pieces	Length		Width		Thickness	
		in.	cm	in.	cm	in.	cm
Base							
Front Leg	2	24⅛	61.28	2¼	5.71	2¼	5.71
Front Leg Halves	4	24⅛	61.28	2	5.08	1⅛	2.86
Front Leg Veneer	4	25⅛	63.36	3¼	8.26	⅛	.32
Back Leg	2	20¼	51.44	2¼	5.71	2¼	5.71
Back Leg Halves	4	20¼	51.44	2	5.08	1⅛	2.86
Back Leg Veneer	4	21¼	53.98	3¼	8.26	⅛	.32
Bottom Side Rail	2	29⅞	75.88	3	7.62	¾	1.91
Top Side Rail	2	26⅞	68.26	3¾	9.54	¾	1.91
Side Slat	10	14½	36.83	3⅝	9.20	½	1.27
Arm							
Arm	2	37	93.98	5	12.70	1	2.54
Arm Support	4	9⅞	25.08	1¾	4.44	1¼	3.17
Rails							
Front Rail	1	28¼	71.76	4½	11.43	¾	1.91
Back Rail	1	28¼	71.76	4	10.16	¾	1.91
Back							
Top Horizontal Back Slat	1	21½	54.61	3⅞	9.84	⅜	.95
		23	58.42				
		(radius)					
Bottom Horizontal Back Slat	4	21½	54.61	2½	6.35	⅜	.95
		23	58 42				
		(radius)					
Post	2	29¼	74.30	1⅝	4.12	1⅛	2.86
Pivot Pin	2	4¾	12.08	1	2.54	1	2.54
Adjustment Pin	2	4¼	12.08	1	2.54	1	2.54
Cleats	2	23¼	59.06	⅝	1.58	1	2.54

⅝-inch (1.58-cm) dowels
⅜-inch (.95-cm) dowels
2 wooden washers
8 steel flathead wood screws

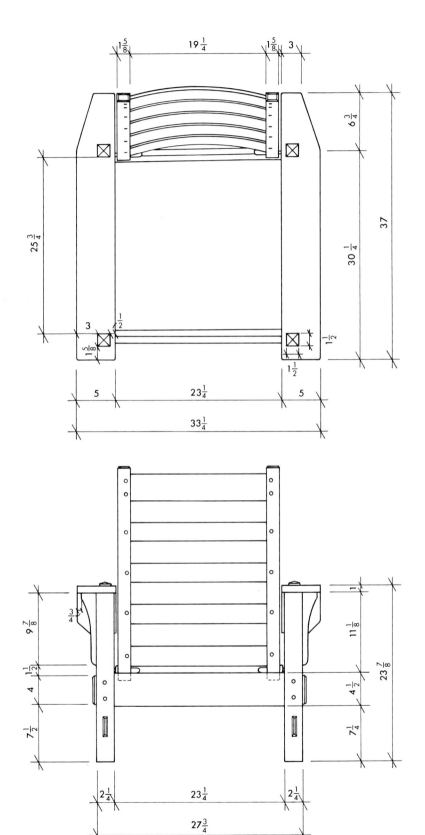

in.	cm
½	1.27
¾	1.91
1½	3.81
1⅝	4.12
2¼	5.71
3	7.62
4	10.16
4½	11.43
5	12.70
6¾	17.14
7¼	18.41
7½	19.05
9⅞	25.08
11⅛	28.25
19¼	48.89
23¼	59.05
23⅞	60.64
25¾	65.40
27¾	70.48
30¼	76.83
33¼	84.45
37	93.98

5-49. Working drawing for recliner. Top and front views and arm support.

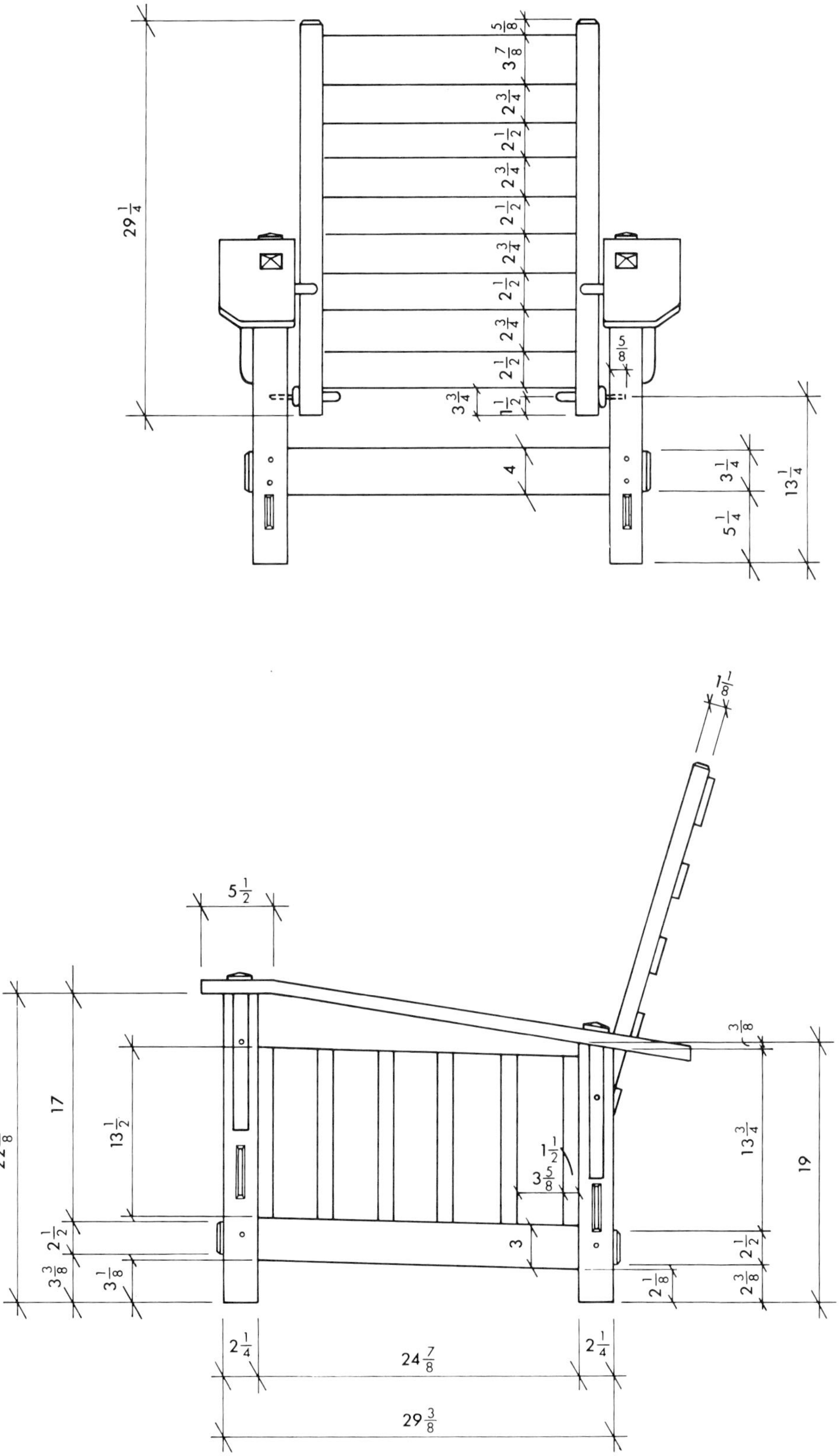

in.	cm
⅜	.95
⅝	1.58
1½	3.81
2⅛	5.39
2¼	5.71
2⅜	6.03
2½	6.35
2¾	6.98
3	7.62
3⅛	7.93
3¼	8.25
3⅜	8.57
3⅝	9.20
3¾	9.52
3⅞	9.84
4	10.16
5¼	13.33
5½	13.97
13¼	33.65
13½	34.29
13¾	34.92
17	43.18
19	48.26
22⅞	58.10
24⅞	63.18
29⅜	74.61
29¼	74.29

5-50. Working drawing for recliner. Back and side views.

PROCEDURE

In addition to the instructions given below, you may need to refer to the general instructions in chapter 4 for the following procedures:

Butt-joining, page 71
Cutting and applying veneer, pages 72–73
Cutting tenons, pages 65–66
Cutting mortises with drill and chisel, page 69
Cutting mortises with router table, pages 76–77
Beveling, page 70
Bending stock, pages 77–78
Cutting tenons on bent stock, pages 66–67
Dowel-pinning, pages 82–83
Constructing seat frame and upholstering, page 88
Finishing, pages 84–87
Assembly, pages 79–83

Side

Base

Each leg is made up of four pieces: two leg halves and two veneer strips. Laminate the leg halves with a butt joint and ⅝-inch (1.58-cm) dowels. The two resulting seams are each covered with a veneer strip. Once the legs are assembled, cut each leg to rough length: the front legs to 24½ inches (62.23 cm) and the back legs to 21 inches (53.34 cm).

Cut a through tenon measuring 1⅝ inches (4.12 cm) long by 1½ inches (3.81 cm) wide by 1½ inches (3.81 cm) thick onto the top of the front leg. Then cut a through tenon measuring 2 inches (5.08 cm) long by 1½ inches (3.81 cm) wide by 1½ inches (3.81) thick onto the top of the back leg. Note that its shoulder must follow the slope of the underside of the arm.

Using the full-size drawing, determine the shoulder angles on the top and bottom side rails and mark.

Cut through tenons on the bottom side rails measuring 2½ inches (6.35 cm) wide by 2¾ inches (6.98 cm) long by ½ inch (1.27 cm) thick. Locate the mortises on both the front and back of each leg, noting the angle of incline shown in the full-size drawing. Cut these mortises using the drill and chisel cleanout method.

Cut blind tenons on the top side rail measuring 2¾ inches (6.98 cm) wide by 1 inch (2.54 cm) long by ½ inch (1.27 cm) thick.

Cut the top edge of the top side rail with a pattern made from the full-size side view drawing using the underside of the arm to determine the angle of the top edge of the top side rail. Allow for a ½ inch (1.27 cm) insertion of the upper edge of the top side rail into a dado to be cut in the underside of the arm.

Locate mortises for the topside rails in the legs and cut them using the drill and chisel cleanout method. Cut blind tenons measuring 2⅝ inches (6.66 cm) wide by ½ inch (1.27 cm) long by ¼ inch (.64 cm) thick on the five side slats. (Note the angle of their shoulders from the full-size side view drawing.) Locate mortise positions for these tenons on the edges of the two bottom side rails and cut using the router table and a ¼-inch (.64-cm) straight bit (figure 5-51).

5-51. Blind mortise and tenon joints connect bottom side rails and slats.

Arm

From the extra length of the arm provided by the oversize dimension given in the materials list, cut a piece 5½ inches (13.97 cm) in length. Place this piece on the bottom side of the arm at the end from which it was cut. This added thickness allows for the change in angle of the front of the arm. Make a pattern of the edge of the arm from the full-size side view drawing. Place this pattern on the edge of the arm and draw its profile. Shade areas to be removed (figure 5-52). Remove the shaded area from the small block with a band saw, holding the wood in a screw clamp. Cut halfway into the block, keeping the blade on the outside edge of the pattern line (figure 5-53). With the block still in the clamp, cut in from the side until you meet your first cut (figure 5-54). Place

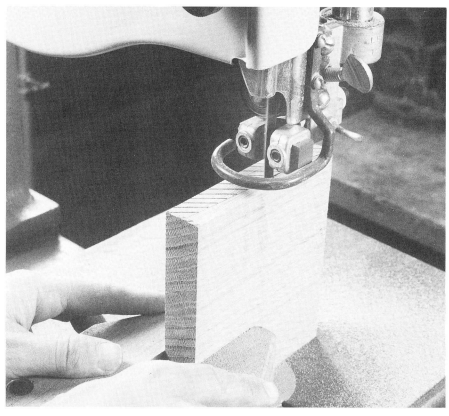

5-53. Using a screw clamp to hold stock, make a cut with a band saw halfway down the stock, cutting on the outside of the pattern line.

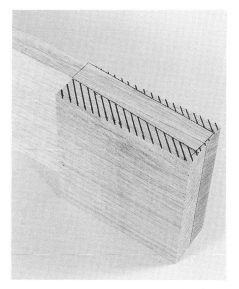

5-52. Block placed on bottom side of arm, shaded areas indicate material to be cut away.

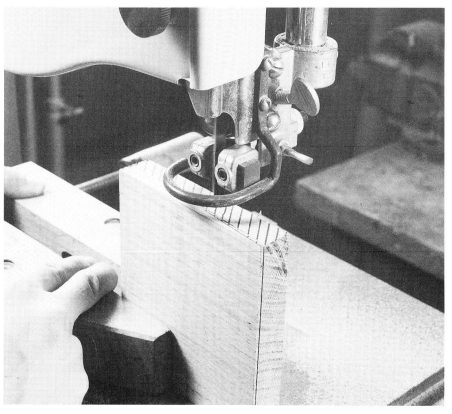

5-54. With stock still in clamp, cut in from the side until you meet your first cut.

123

5–55. Place cut end in clamp and finish removing material by cutting from the opposite end.

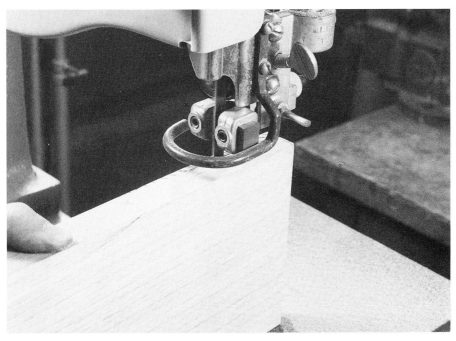

5–56. Cut the waste material from the top side of the arm.

the end from which material has been cut into the clamp and finish removing shaded area from the opposite end (figure 5-55). Cut the shaded area from the top of the arm (figure 5-56). Laminate the block to the arm, using four C-clamps (figure 5-57). After the arm lamination is dry, remove any saw marks from the top and underside with a sanding block (figure 5-58).

Locate the mortises in the arm that will receive the through tenons already cut on the top of each leg (figure 5-49). (Note in figure 5-59 that the mortises for the back legs' tenons are cut at an angle.) Cut these using the drill and chisel cleanout method.

Dado the underside of the arm ¾ inch (1.91 cm) from the inside edge to a depth of ½ inch (1.27 cm) using a router with a ¾-inch (1.91-cm) straight bit and then a drill with a ¾ inch (1.91 cm) forstner or boring bit. Use the router, with the aid of a fence, to cut the dado from the back mortise to just behind the bend in the arm. Then use the drill to make a series of holes from that point to the front mortise. Chisel clean to form the complete dado, as shown in figure 5-60.

Drill four ⅝-inch (1.58-cm) holes 2¼ inches (5.71 cm) deep in the back inside edge of each arm to hold adjusting pins. Locate the first hole 1½ inches (3.81 cm), on center, from the end of the arm; space the remaining holes 1¼ inches (3.17 cm) away, on center, from the preceding hole.

Cut the back edge of the arm to the profile shown in the top view drawing (figure 5-49).

5-57. Using four C-clamps, laminate the two sections together.

5-58. Finished arm.

5-59. Using a drill press with its table adjusted to the angle needed, drill out excess material to create mortise in arm for back leg tenon.

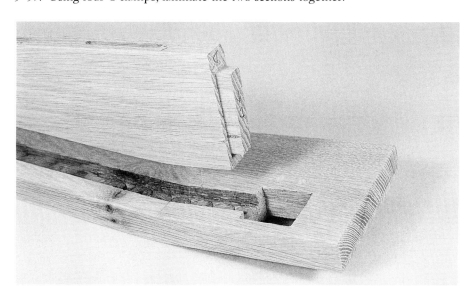

5-60. Dado cut in the bottom side of the arm holds the top side rail.

Rails

Cut the through tenons on the front and back rails that will join the two side assemblies. The tenons on the front rail should measure 4 inches (10.16 cm) wide by 2½ inches (6.35 cm) long by ½ inch (1.27 cm) thick. The tenons on the back rail should measure 3¼ inches (8.26 cm) wide by 2½ inches (6.35 cm) long by ½ inch (1.27 cm) thick. Locate the mortises for these tenons on the legs (see figures 5-49 and 5-50) and cut, using the drill and chisel cleanout method.

Subassembly

Final preparation of all through tenon ends is necessary prior to assembly. All through tenon ends project ¼ inch (.64 cm) beyond their exit point. Bevel the ends of all through *rail* tenons with a disc sander or block plane according to guidelines placed ³/₁₆ inch (.47 cm) down from the end along each side and ⅛ inch (.32 cm) in from each edge on the end. Bevel the ends of all through *leg* tenons beginning 1¹/₁₆ inches (2.69 cm) from the shoulder and meeting in the center to form a peak.

Assemble each side independently. When both sides are dry after gluing, join them together with the front and back rails.

Cut arm supports on a band saw or jigsaw, using a pattern adapted from figure 5-49. Sand and shape supports on the drill press with a drum sanding attachment. Sand and fit the bevel on the rear arm supports to contour to the slope of the rear portion of the arm. Glue each arm support in place so that they touch the underside of the arm and are centered on the leg.

5–61. Back assembly, clamped. Notched wood pads hold the bar and C-clamps in place. Assemble the back on two boards, bridging tables, or stools to aid in positioning bar and C-clamps.

Back

Bend the horizontal slats using the procedure described in chapter 4.

Cut blind tenons on the bent slats with either a band saw or backsaw. The top back slat tenons should measure 2⅞ inches (7.30 cm) wide by 1 inch (2.54 cm) long by ¼ inch (.64 cm) thick. The four remaining slats should have tenons measuring 1½ inches (3.81 cm) wide by 1 inch (2.54 cm) long by ¼ inch (.64 cm) thick.

Locate the mortises, on center, on the inside edge of each post (see figure 5-50). Cut each mortise using the drill and chisel cleanout method.

Drill a ⅝-inch (1.58-cm) hole, on center, 1½ inches (3.81 cm) from the bottom of each post. Drill from the inside edge of each post completely through the post. Drill the same size hole on the inside surface of each leg, 13¼ inches (33.66 cm) on center from the bottom of the leg, to a depth of 2 inches (5.08 cm). These holes will accommodate the pivot pins for the back.

Assembly

Assemble the back as indicated in figure 5-61. Because the back slats will flex during clamping, use additional clamps to counteract this and to ensure a proper seam line between the shoulder of each back slat and the post. Attach these clamps with wooden pads notched to fit over the bar clamps holding the posts and slats together.

All tenons can now be pinned with ⅜-inch (.95-cm) dowels. Insert the lower side rail dowels in the centers of the legs, centered on the tenons. Pin the front rail tenons with two dowels on each leg. Locate the lower dowel 8¼ inches

(21.5 cm), on center, from the bottom of the leg, and the upper dowel 10¾ inches (27.32 cm), on center, from the bottom of the leg. Pin the back rail tenons in the same manner as those for the front rail, with the lower dowel 6 inches (15.24 cm), on center, from the bottom of the leg and the upper dowel 8¼ inches (21.5 cm) on center, from the bottom of the leg.

To pin the through tenons on the top of each leg, center the dowel on the inside edge of the arm, centered on the tenon. Pin the arm supports 5½ inches

(13.97 cm), on center, from the bottom of the support. Pin the top back slat with two dowels on each tenon, ¾ inch (1.9 cm) from the inside edge of each post. Locate the upper dowel 1⅝ inches (4.12 cm), on center from the top of the post and the lower dowel 3⅜ inches (8.5 cm), on center, from the top of the post. Pin the four lower back slats with one dowel in each tenon, ⅜ inch (.95 cm) from the inside edge of the post, centered on each tenon.

Use a lathe to turn the pivot and adjustment pins according to the dimensions in figure 5-62.

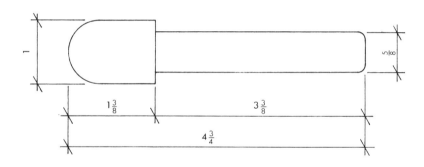

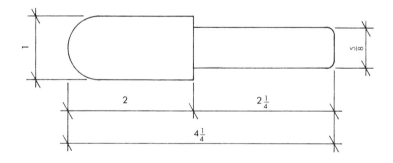

in.	cm
⅝	1.58
1	2.54
1⅜	3.49
2	5.08
2¼	5.71
3⅜	8.57
4¼	10.80

5-62. Working drawings for pivot and adjustment pins. The top is the pivot pin; the bottom is the adjustment pin.

5–63. Pivot and adjustment pins in position.

Make wooden washers for the pivot pins by first laminating two pieces of ⅛-inch-thick (.32-cm) stock with their grains perpendicular. Cut two 1-inch (2.54-cm) squares from this laminated stock. Find the center of each square and, with a compass, draw two concentric circles with diameters of ⅝ inch (1.58 cm) and 1 inch (2.54 cm). Drill a ⅝-inch (1.58-cm) hole in the center of the square. With a disc sander or file, round the outside corners to the 1-inch circle line. Round the outside edges with a file and sandpaper.

Braces called cleats are used to support the seat frame. These cleats measure ⅝ inch (1.58 cm) thick by 23¼ inches (59.06 cm) long by 1 inch (2.54 cm) wide. Place the 1-inch (2.54-cm) dimensions of the cleats against the inside surfaces of the front and back rails, 1½ inches (3.81 cm) down from the top edge. Glue each cleat to its rail. Strengthen them with four wood screws in each cleat.

Apply a finish to the piece using the procedure described in chapter 4.

You have now completed construction of the recliner. Information for construction of the seat frame and upholstery is given in chapter 4.

Settle

Stickley designed the settle or couch for lounging. Quite unlike the Victorian sofa, the settle encouraged one to relax, while the Victorian piece had an air of formality that almost demanded a prim, upright posture. Each settle was designed to be used with throw pillows instead of an upholstered back, thereby offering versatile seating to accommodate anyone.

5-66. Exploded view of settle.

MATERIALS

	Number of Pieces	Length		Width		Thickness	
		in.	cm	in.	cm	in.	cm
Legs							
Leg	4	29	73.66	2¾	6.98	2¾	6.98
Leg Halves	8	29	73.66	2½	6.35	1⅜	3.49
Leg Veneer	8	30	76.20	3¼	8.26	⅛	.32
Rails							
Bottom Side Rail	2	32	81.28	5	12.70	⅞	2.22
Top Side Rail	2	30½	77.47	5	12.70	⅞	2.22
Front Rail	1	76½	194.31	6½	16.51	⅞	2.22
Bottom Back Rail	1	76½	194.31	6½	16.51	⅞	2.22
Top Back Rail	1	73½	186.69	5	12.70	⅞	2.22
Slats							
Side Slat	6	17¼	43.82	6	15.24	⅜	.95
Back Slat	8	12	30.48	6	15.24	⅜	.95
Cleats							
Cleat	2	70½	179.07	1¾	4.44	1	2.54

⅜-inch (.95-cm) dowels
⅝-inch (1.58-cm) dowels
16 steel flathead wood screws

The settle is a relatively easy piece to construct because it contains only mortise-and-tenon joinery. Two subassemblies are required to build the settle: each side is assembled independently. The sides are then connected by three rails, one in the front and two at the back. The sides are identical; each consists of two legs, two side rails, and three vertical side slats. Eight vertical slats connect the top and bottom back rails. Cut your stock according to the dimensions given in the materials list.

5–67. Settle.

in.	cm	in.	cm
½	1.27	6¼	15.87
2½	6.35	6½	16.51
2¾	6.98	6¾	17.14
5	12.70	10¾	52.70
5½	13.97	70½	179.07
6	15.24	76	193.04

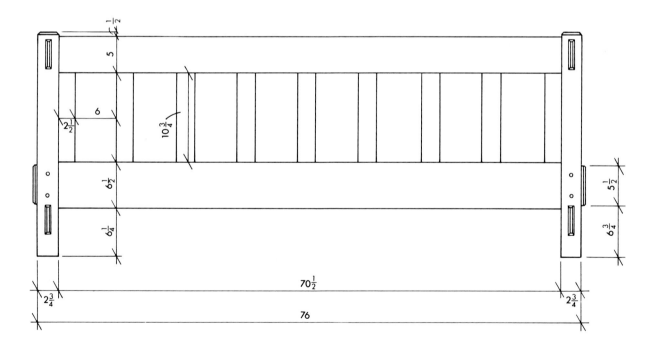

5-68. Working drawing for settle. Top and back views. (See figure 5-70 for detail of circled area.)

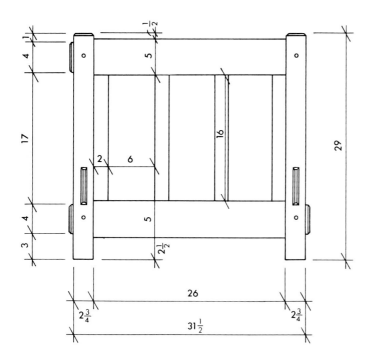

in.	cm
½	1.27
1	2.54
2	5.08
2½	6.35
2¾	6.93
3	7.62
4	10.16
5	12.70
6	15.24
16	40.64
17	43.18
26	66.04
29	73.66
31½	80.01

5-69. Working drawing for settle. Side view.

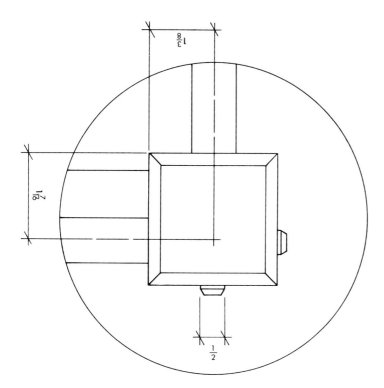

in.	cm
½	1.27
1⅜	3.49
1⁷⁄₁₆	3.65

5-70. Detail showing location of side, front, and back rails on legs.

PROCEDURE

In addition to the instructions given below, you may need to refer to the general instructions in chapter 4 for the following procedures:

Butt-joining, page 71
Cutting and applying veneer, pages 72–73
Beveling, page 70
Cutting tenons, pages 65–66
Cutting mortises with drill and chisel, page 69
Cutting mortises with router, pages 76–77
Dowel-pinning, pages 82–83
Assembly, pages 79–83
Constructing seat frame and upholstering, page 88
Finishing, pages 84–87

Legs

Each leg is made up of four pieces: two leg halves and two veneer strips. Laminate the leg halves with a butt joint, using ⅝-inch (1.58-cm) dowels. Cover the two resulting seams on each leg with veneer strips. Cut each leg to length.

Bevel the top of each leg with a disc sander or a block and sandpaper. Cut this bevel according to guidelines drawn ¼ inch (.64 cm) down from the top edge on each side and ¼ (.64 cm) in from all edges on the top.

Rails

Cut through tenons measuring 4 inches (10.16 cm) wide by 3 inches (7.62 cm) long by ½ inch (1.27 cm) thick on both ends of the bottom side rails. Cut a through tenon measuring 4 inches (10.16 cm) wide by 3 inches (7.62 cm) long by ½ inch (1.27 cm) thick on the *front* ends of the top

side rails. Cut a blind tenon measuring 4 inches (10.16 cm) wide by 1½ inches (3.81 cm) long by ½ inch (1.27 cm) thick on the *back* ends of the top side rails.

Locate the mortises for these tenons (see figure 5-68); center the mortises on each leg (figure 5-70). Cut them using the drill and chisel cleanout method.

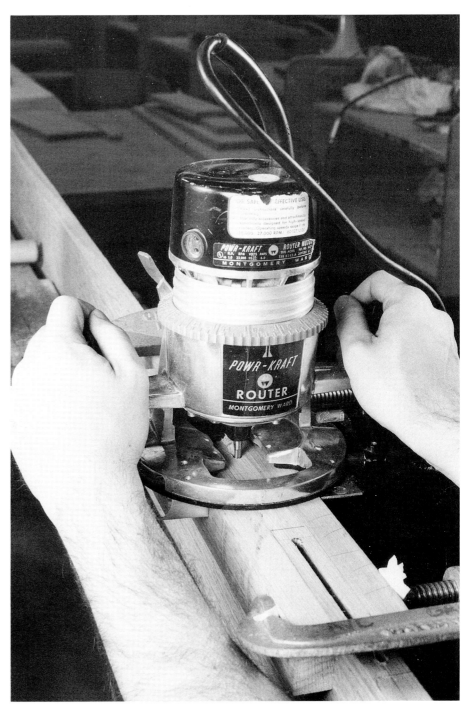

5-71. Cut mortises in rail using router. Clamp boards to each side of the rail to support the router base plate.

Cut the front and bottom back rail through tenons to measure 5½ inches (13.97 cm) wide by 3 inches (7.62 cm) long by ½ inch (1.27 cm) thick. Cut the back top rail blind tenons measuring 4 inches (10.16 cm) wide by 1½ inches (3.81 cm) long by ½ inch (1.27 cm) thick.

Locate mortise centers for the front and both back rails 1⁷⁄₁₆ inches (3.65 cm) from the inside leg corner (see figures 5-69 and 5-70). The top back rail mortise begins 1 inch (2.54 cm) down from the top of the leg. Cut these mortises using the drill and chisel cleanout method.

Slats

Cut blind tenons measuring 5 inches (12.70 cm) wide by ⅝ inches (1.58 cm) long by ¼ inch (.64 cm) thick on the six vertical side slats. Locate the mortises (see figure 5-69) and center them on the top edge of the bottom side rail and the bottom edge of the top side rail. Cut the mortises with

a router and a ¼-inch (.64-cm) straight bit, using a support jig, as shown in figure 5-71.

Cut blind tenons measuring 5 inches (12.70 cm) wide by ⅝ inch (1.58 cm) long by ¼ inch (.64 cm) thick on the eight vertical back slats. Locate and cut the mortises on the back rails using the same measurements and procedure as on the side rails.

Assembly

Bevel all through tenons with a disc sander or block plane. Bevel according to guidelines drawn ³⁄₁₆ inch (.47 cm) down from the end along each side and ⅛ inch (.32 cm) in from each edge on the end.

Glue each side subassembly together. When both sides are dry, connect them with the front and back rails. Remember, the back slats must be glued in place at the same time that the front and back rails are assembled with the sides.

Pin all rail tenons with ⅜-inch (.95-cm) dowels. Locate the dowels for the top and bottom side

rails and the top back rail in the center of the leg, centered on the tenon. Pin the front and bottom back rail tenons with two dowels each. Locate both dowels in the center of the leg, the lower dowel, 8 ¼ inches (20.96 cm), on center, from the bottom of the leg, and the upper dowel, 10 ¾ inches (27.31 cm), on center, from the bottom of the leg.

Braces called cleats are used to support the seat frame. Place their 1¾-inch (4.44-cm) dimension against the inside surfaces of the front and bottom back rails, 1¾ inches (4.44 cm) down from the top edge of each rail. Glue each cleat to its rail. Strengthen them with eight wood screws in each cleat.

Apply a finish to the piece using the procedure described in chapter 4.

You have now completed the settle. Information for construction of the seat frame and upholstery is given in chapter 4.

Dining Table

The dining table is one piece of furniture designed to be used simultaneously by the entire family. In most families it functions as more than just a dining surface: it also provides a forum for discussing the events of the day. Of the dining tables designed and built by Stickley, this table most typifies his belief in traditional structural systems. That most basic of structural systems, the post and lintel, forms the support for the massive top. The construction of the table is simple; because of its massiveness, however, you will require assistance during some construction procedures.

This dining table requires three subassemblies: two identical leg units that consist of two legs, a bottom rail, and a top horizontal support, which are connected after subassembly by a stretcher; and a laminated top.

5-73. Exploded view of dining table.

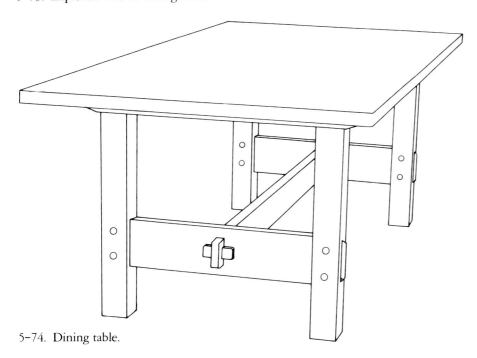

5-74. Dining table.

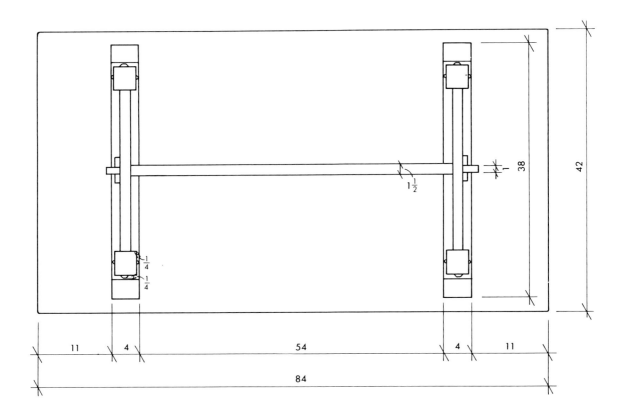

in.	cm	in.	cm	in.	cm
¼	.64	3⅜	8.57	38	96.52
¾	1.91	3½	8.89	42	106.68
1	2.54	4	10.16	54	137.16
1½	3.81	4½	11.43	54½	138.43
2½	6.35	6½	16.51	84	213.36

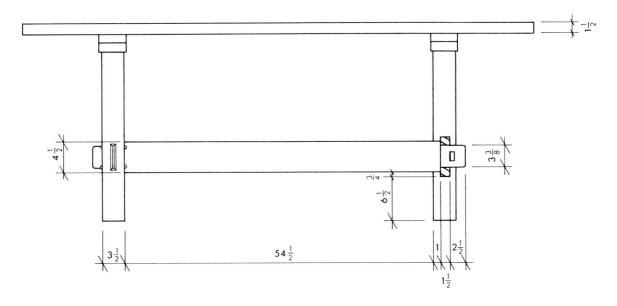

5-75. Working drawing for dining table. Bottom and side views.

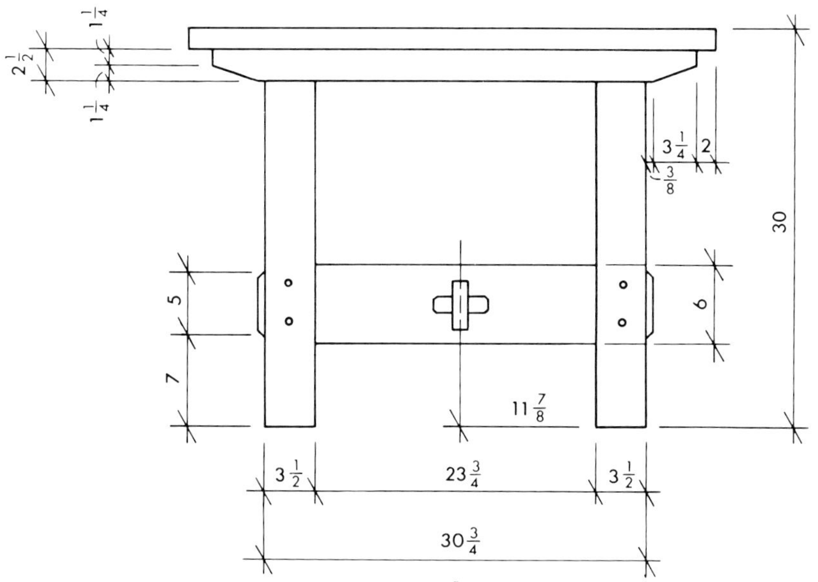

in.	cm
¼	.64
⅜	.95
1¼	3.17
2	5.08
2½	6.35
3¼	8.25
3½	8.89
5	12.70
6	15.24
7	17.78
11⅞	30.16
23¾	60.32
30	76.20
30¾	78.10

5-76. Working drawing for dining table. End view.

MATERIALS

	Number of Pieces	Length		Width		Thickness	
		in.	cm	in.	cm	in.	cm
Leg Units							
Leg	4	28	71.12	3½	8.89	3½	8.89
Leg Halves	8	28	71.12	3¼	8.26	1¾	4.44
Leg Veneer	8	29	73.66	4½	11.43	⅛	.32
Horizontal Top Support	2	38	96.52	4	10.16	2½	6.35
Bottom Rail	2	31¼	79.38	6	15.24	1½	3.81
Stretcher	1	64½	163.83	4½	11.43	1½	3.81
Key	2	3⅞	9.84	1⅜	3.49	¾	1.91
Table Top							
Top	1	84	213.36	42	106.68	1½	3.81
Caps	16	1	2.54			¾ (diam.)	1.91

⅝-inch (1.58-cm) dowels
14 1¼-inch (3.17-cm) table irons
28 flathead wood screws

PROCEDURE

In addition to the instructions given below, you may need to refer to the general instructions in chapter 4 for the following procedures:

Butt-joining, page 71
Cutting and applying veneer, pages 72–73
Cutting tenons, pages 65–66
Beveling, page 70
Cutting mortises with drill and chisel, page 69
Dowel-pinning, pages 82–83
Squaring laminated boards, pages 74–75
Assembly, pages 79–83
Finishing, pages 84–87

Leg Units

Legs

Each leg is composed of two halves and two veneer strips. Laminate the leg halves with butt joints, using ⅝-inch (1.58-cm) dowels. Cover the resulting seams with the veneer strips. After veneering, cut the legs to length, allowing for a 2-inch-long (5.08-cm) blind tenon on the top of each.

Cut blind tenons measuring 1½ inches (3.81 cm) wide by 2 inches (5.08 cm) long by 1½ inches (3.81 cm) thick on the top of each leg (figure 5-77).

Horizontal Top Supports

Laminate the horizontal supports with ⅝-inch (1.58-cm) dowels. Bevel their bottom corners as shown in figure 5-76. Locate mortises for the blind tenons on the legs (see figure 5-76). Cut mortises in the underside of the top horizontal supports using the drill and chisel cleanout method (figure 5-77).

5-77. Blind mortise-and-tenon joint connects leg and horizontal top support.

5-78. Mortise and tenon join rail and leg.

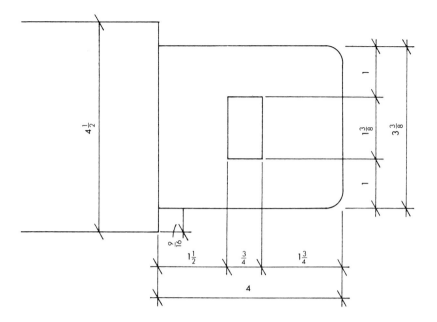

5-79. Working drawing for stretcher tenon and its mortise.

in.	cm
9/16	1.43
3/4	1.91
1	2.54
1 3/8	3.49
1 1/2	3.81
1 3/4	4.44
3 3/8	8.57
4	10.16
4 1/2	11.43

Rails

Cut through tenons measuring 5 inches (12.70 cm) wide by 3¼ inches (8.26 cm) long by 1 inch (2.54 cm) thick on both ends of each rail. Locate mortises in the center of each leg (see figure 5-76), and cut, using the drill and chisel cleanout method (figure 5-78)

Final preparation of the rail tenon ends is necessary prior to subassembly. Bevel the tenon ends, which project 5/16 inch (.79 cm) beyond their exit points, with a disc sander or block plane. Use guidelines placed ¼ inch (.64 cm) down from the end along each side and ¼ inch (.64 cm) in from each edge on the end of the tenon.

Stretcher

Cut through tenons measuring 3⅜ inches (8.57 cm) wide by 4 inches (10.16 cm) long by 1 inch (2.54 cm) thick on each end of the stretcher. Round the tenon ends as shown in figure 5-79, and lightly bevel the shaded area with a medium crosscut file. Locate mortises for the tenons in the center of each rail. Cut using the drill and chisel cleanout method.

The stretcher tenons will be locked in place with keys inserted through mortises cut in the end of

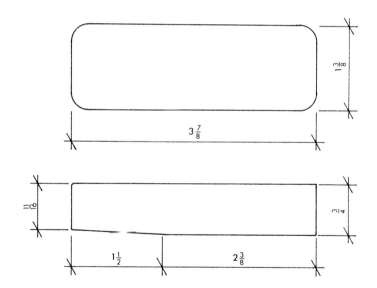

5-80. Working drawing for key.

in.	cm
11/16	1.75
3/4	1.91
1 3/8	3.49
1 1/2	3.81
2 3/8	6.03
3 7/8	9.84

each tenon. To locate the mortises for the keys, insert the stretcher tenons into their mortises in the rails. Draw a pencil line around each tenon at the point where it exits the rail. Remove the tenons from the rails. The pencil lines indicate the edge of the key mortises closest to the rail.

Locate the other three sides of each mortise (figure 5-79), and cut with the drill and chisel clean-out method. Cut the keys on a band saw or jigsaw (figure 5-80) and shape with a file, block plane, or sanding block. Care should be taken in fitting each key exactly to its mortise.

Subassembly

Set the horizontal top support in place (not glued) to maintain leg alignment while gluing the rails. Glue the rails into the legs. When the glue is dry, assemble the horizontal top support with glue and clamp.

After the leg units are assembled, pin the rail tenons with two ⅝-inch (1.58-cm) dowels on each, as shown in figure 5-81. The dowels are recessed to accommodate caps, which can be turned to the size indicated on a lathe or shaped from ¾-inch (1.91-cm) diameter oak dowel using a flat, medium crosscut file.

Tabletop

The table is laminated from five to seven pieces of stock, depending upon the stock widths available. Lay out the top, being careful to alternate end grain direction or pattern so as to minimize the warping so characteristic of large, solid tabletops. Butt-join the boards edge-to-edge with ⅝-inch (1.58-cm) dowels. Assemble the boards in pairs first, because of the massiveness of the top.

After tabletop assembly is complete, use a router to trim one end square. Measure the top to length and trim the other end. Round the corners with a medium crosscut file using a ½ inch radius template as a guide.

Assembly

Attach the two leg units to the stretcher. Glue the keys into place. Seven evenly spaced table irons are used on each horizontal top support, four on one side, three on the other. With a 1-inch (2.54-cm) forstner or boring bit, countersink each table iron flush with the top of the horizontal support. Secure the irons with flathead wood screws.

Apply a finish to the piece. Place the tabletop in position. Secure it with steel flathead screws driven through the table iron into the underside of the top.

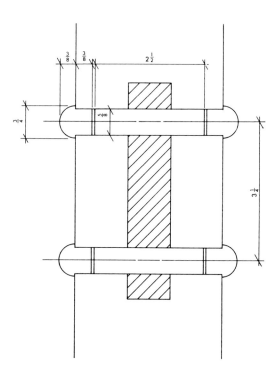

in.	cm
⅜	.95
⅝	1.58
¾	1.91
2½	6.35
3¼	8.25

5-81. Working drawing showing location of ⅝-inch (1.58-cm) dowels and their caps.

Bookcase

Although this bookcase is one of the projects from the Home Training in Cabinet-Work series in *The Craftsman*, it is not a simple piece to build. The bookcase is not technically difficult, but because of the number of pieces, extensive joinery, and critical alignment requirements involved, it requires much time and patience.

5-83. Exploded view of bookcase showing sides, doors, shelves, and front bottom rail.

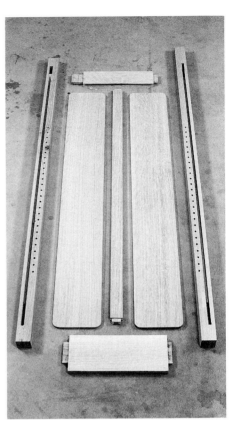

5-85. Exploded view of bookcase side.

5-84. Exploded view of bookcase showing sides, back rails, and back panels.

5-86. Exploded view of bookcase door.

The bookcase has four sub-assemblies: two identical side units and two identical doors. Each side unit consits of seven pieces: two posts, a top and a bottom side rail, a center vertical side rail, and two panels. The accurate milling of the two posts is essential to proper alignment of the parts they join. The two side units are connected by the back and by a front bottom rail to form the bookcase's frame. The frame contains three permanent shelves, at the top, middle, and bottom. The second sub-assemblies, the two doors, each consist of eight pieces: two stiles, a top and a bottom door rail, one horizontal mullion, and three vertical mullions. Each door is connected to the frame with hinges. Cut your stock according to the dimensions given in the materials list.

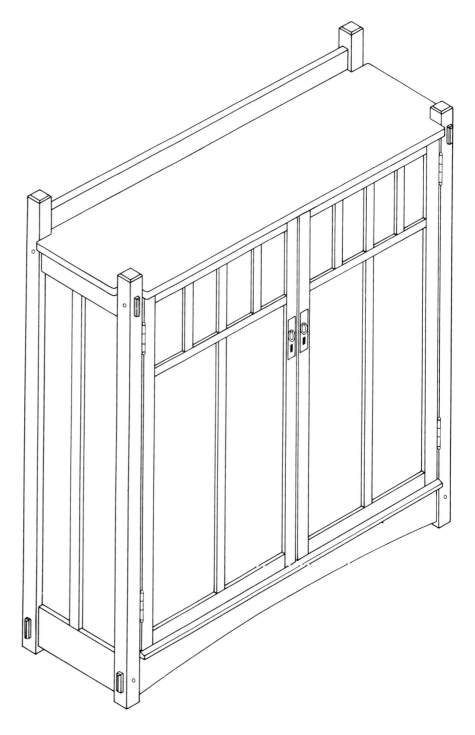

5–87. Bookcase.

MATERIALS

	Number of Pieces	Length in.	Length cm	Width in.	Width cm	Thickness in.	Thickness cm
Side Units							
Bottom Side Rail	2	12¾	32.40	4½	11.43	¾	1.91
Front Post	2	51	161.94	1¾	4.44	1¾	4.44
Back Post	2	54	137.16	1¾	4.44	1¾	4.44
Top Side Rail	2	14¾	37.48	3½	8.89	¾	1.91
Center Vertical Side Rail	2	41¾	106.06	1½	3.81	¾	1.91
Side Panel	4	41¼	104.78	6	15.24	½	1.27
Shelves							
Top Shelf	1	46¾	118.76	14⅛	35.88	¾	1.91
Middle Shelf	1	44	111.76	12	30.48	¾	1.91
Bottom Shelf	1	44	111.76	14⅛	35.88	¾	1.91
Front Bottom Rail							
Front Bottom Rail	1	46¼	117.48	4½	11.43	¾	1.91
Back							
Back Bottom Rail	1	46¼	117.48	3	7.62	¾	1.91
Top Back Rail	1	44¾	113.68	2½	6.35	¾	1.91
Back Panel	5	46¼	117.48	9	22.86	½	1.27
Spline	4	46¼	117.48	1	2.54	⅛	.32
Doors							
Door Stile	4	42⅜	107.63	1½	3.81	¾	1.91
Door Rail	4	20	50.80	1½	3.81	¾	1.91
Horizontal Mullion	2	20	50.80	1	2.54	¾	1.91
Center Vertical Mullion	2	41⅜	105.09	1	2.54	¾	1.91
Side Vertical Mullion	4	8¾	22.23	1	2.54	¾	1.91
Stops							
Top and Bottom Door Stops	2	2	5.08	½	1.27	½	1.27
Hinge Supports	2	42⅜	107.63	½	1.27	1	2.54
Glass							
Outside Panes	4	8¹¹⁄₁₆	22.07	4⁷⁄₁₆	11.27	⅛	.32
Inside Panes	4	8¹¹⁄₁₆	22.07	4³⁄₁₆	10.63	⅛	.32
Lower Panes	4	31¹⁄₁₆	78.89	9³⁄₁₆	23.33	⅛	.32

⅜-inch (.95-cm) dowels
4 loose-pin brass or steel box hinges
2 door pulls
1 spring-action cupboard latch
1 small cupboard lock
2 molding strips, 25 feet (7.62 m) by ¼ inch (.64 cm) by ⅜ inch (.95 cm)
brads

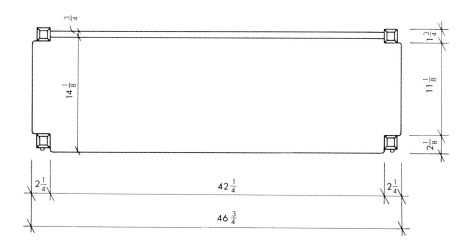

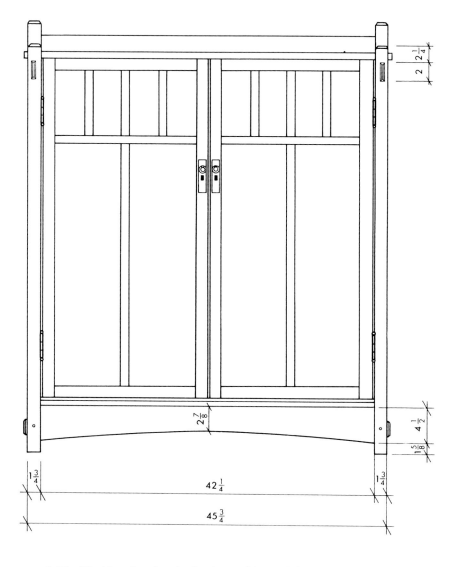

in.	cm
¾	1.91
1⅝	4.12
1¾	4.44
2	5.08
2⅛	5.39
2¼	5.71
2⅞	7.30
4½	11.43
11⅛	28.25
14⅛	35.87
42¼	107.31
45¾	116.20
46¾	118.74

5-88. Working drawing for bookcase. Top and front views.

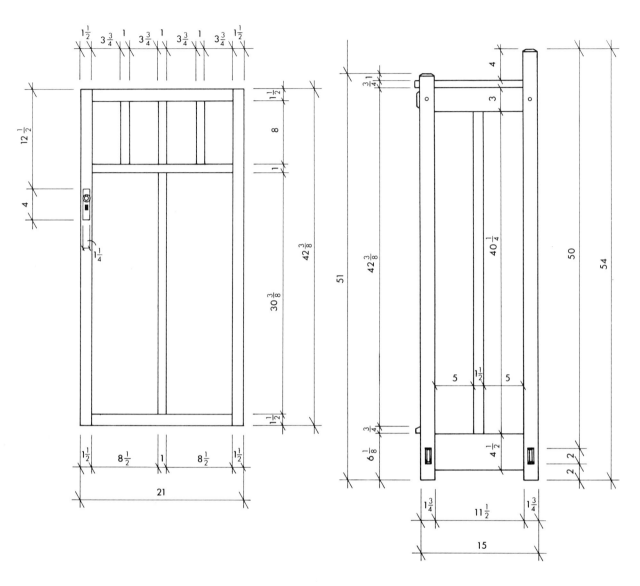

5-89. Working drawing for bookcase. Door and side view.

in.	cm		in.	cm
¾	1.91		8	20.32
1	2.54		8½	21.59
1¼	3.17		11½	29.21
1½	3.81		12½	31.75
1¾	4.44		15	38.10
2	5.08		21	53.34
3	7.62		30⅜	77.15
3¾	9.52		40¼	102.23
4	10.16		42⅜	107.63
4½	11.43		50	127.00
5	12.70		51	129.54
6⅛	15.55		54	137.16

PROCEDURE

In addition to the instructions given below, you may need to refer to the general instructions in chapter 4 for the following procedures:

Cutting tenons, pages 65–66
Cutting mortises with drill and chisel, page 69
Constructing and using a router table, pages 75–76
Butt-joining, page 71
Squaring laminated boards, pages 74–75
Beveling, page 70
Dowel-pinning, pages 82–83
Cutting barefaced tenons, pages 67–68
Treating hinges, page 88
Attaching hinges, page 88
Assembly, pages 79–83
Finishing, pages 84–87

Frame

Side Units

Cut blind tenons measuring 3½ inches (8.89 cm) wide by ⅝ inch (1.58 cm) long by ½ inch (1.27 cm) thick on each end of the bottom side rail. Locate the mortises on the posts; draw the mortises' center lines ⅜ inch (.95 cm) in from the outside edges of the posts and the bottom of the mortise 2 inches (5.08 cm) from the bottom of the post. Cut the mortises using the drill and chisel cleanout method.

The top side rails each have a blind tenon at the back and a through tenon at the front. Tenons begin 1 inch (2.54 cm) from the top edge of each rail. Cut the blind tenon to measure 2 inches (5.08 cm) wide by 1¼ inches (3.17 cm) long by ½ inch (1.27 cm) thick. Then cut the through tenon to measure 2 inches (5.08 cm)

wide by 2 inches (5.08 cm) long by ½ inch (1.27 cm) thick. Locate the mortises ⅜ inch (.95 cm), on center, from the outside post edge on the front and back posts. The front post mortise begins 2¼ inches (5.71 cm) from the top of the front post. The back post mortise begins 5¼ inches (13.33 cm) from the top of the back post. Cut the mortises using the drill and chisel cleanout method.

Cut blind tenons measuring 1 inch (2.54 cm) wide by ¾ inch (1.91 cm) long by ⅝ inch (1.58 cm) thick on each end of the center vertical rail. Locate and cut mortises for this rail in the center of the top edge of the bottom side rail and the bottom edge of the top side rail, using the drill and chisel cleanout method (see figures 5-85 and 5-89).

Round the corners of each side panel to aid in assembly.

Using the router table and a ½-inch (1.27-cm) straight bit, cut a ½-inch-wide (1.27-cm) dado ½ inch (1.27 cm) into the posts, aligning with and connecting the mortises for the top and bottom side rails (see figure 5-85). Cut the same size dado —½ inch (1.27 cm) wide by ½ inch (1.27 cm) deep—centered, on the top edge of the bottom side rail and the bottom edge of the top side rail. Cut the same dado, on center, on both edges of the center vertical side rail. These dados extend the full length of each rail and will accommodate the side panels.

Front Bottom Rail

Cut through tenons measuring 2 inches (5.08 cm) wide by 2 inches (5.08 cm) long by ½ inch (1.27 cm) thick on each end of the front bottom rail. These tenons are *not* centered on the front bottom rail, but begin ½ inch (1.27

cm) up from the bottom edge.

Cut the pattern or arc in the bottom edge of the front rail using a band saw. Remember that the center measurement given in figure 5-88 is from the underside of the shelf, not from the top edge of the rail. Because the front bottom rail will be inserted into a ½-inch-deep (1.27-cm) dado to be cut in the bottom shelf, the center measurement from the top to bottom edge of the rail should be 3⅜ inches (8.57 cm) and the measurement at each end should be 5 inches (12.7 cm). Sand clean on a drill press using a drum sanding attachment.

Locate and cut mortises centered on the front posts using the drill and chisel cleanout method.

Back

Cut through tenons measuring 2 inches (5.08 cm) wide by 2 inches (5.08 cm) long by ½ inch (1.27 cm) thick on both ends of the back bottom rail. Locate and cut mortises into the back posts in the same position as those mortises for the front bottom rail that were cut on the front posts, using the drill and chisel cleanout method.

Cut blind tenons measuring 1½ inches (3.81 cm) wide by 1 inch (2.54 cm) long by ½ inch (1.27 cm) thick on both ends of the top back rail. Cut mortises, on center, on the inside of the back post, beginning 2½ inches (6.35 cm) down from the top the posts; use the drill and chisel cleanout method.

The body of the back is constructed of five oak plywood panels joined along their edges with splines. Using the table saw, cut a ⅛-inch-wide (.32-cm) dado, ½ inch (1.27 cm) deep, into the inside edge of the two end panels

149

and into both edges of the three remaining panels. After the dados have been cut, slightly bevel the edges of each panel on both sides with a sanding block. You may need to remove a triangular sliver from the top and bottom corners of the end panels to provide a proper fit into the posts (see figure 5-84).

Using the router table and a ½-inch (1.27-cm) straight bit, cut a ½-inch-wide (1.27-cm) dado ½ inch (1.27 cm) deep, on center, into each back post for insertion of the end panels of the back. This dado should connect the mortises of the top and bottom back rails. Cut a ½-inch-wide (1.27-cm) dado ½ inch (1.27 cm) deep into the center of the bottom edge of the top back rail and the center of the top edge of the back bottom rail. These dados extend the full length of each rail.

Shelves

If you plan to add additional shelves to the bookcase, drill ¼-inch (.64-cm) holes for adjustable peg shelf supports parallel to the side panel dados on the front and back posts. Locate the bottom hole 8 inches (20.32 cm), on center, from the bottom of the post. Drill the remaining twenty-five holes at 1-inch (2.54-cm) intervals. Drill all holes to a depth of ¾ inch (1.91 cm).

Laminate the bottom, center, and top shelves by butt-joining two or three pieces (depending on stock width) of stock edge-to-edge with ⅜-inch (.95-cm) diameter dowels. Lay out the shelves, being careful to alternate the end grain direction of the boards to minimize warping.

Trim the laminated shelf ends with a router. First trim one end square, measure to length, and

then trim the other end.

Notch the top shelf to fit around the four posts using the dimensions given in figure 5-88, top view. Round the corners indicated in the drawing with a ¼-inch (.64-cm) radius template as a guide.

Locate and cut ¾-inch wide, (1.91-cm) ½-inch deep (1.27-cm) dados, beginning ¾ inch (1.91 cm) from each side end of the bottom surface of the top shelf, using a router and fence and a ¾-inch (1.91-cm) straight bit. This dado fits over the top edge of the top side rails, locking the shelf in place.

Cut ¾-inch-long (1.91-cm) notches into the inside corners of each post to hold the middle shelf in place. Locate the notches in the back post ⅞ inch (2.22 cm) in from the inside surface and ¼ inch (.64 cm) in from the front surface of the back post. Locate the notches in the front posts ⅞ inch (2.22 cm) in from the inside surface and ¼ inch (.64) in from the back surface of the front post. The back post notches begin 14¼ inches (36.20 cm) down from the top of each post, and front post notches begin 11¼ inches (28.58 cm) down from the top of each post.

Cut ¾-inch-long (1.91-cm) notches into the inside corners of each back post to hold the bottom shelf in place. These notches have the same dimensions as those for the middle shelf. Begin each notch 6⅛ inches (15.56 cm) up from the bottom of each post. Cut a ¾-inch-wide (1.91-cm), ½-inch-deep (1.27-cm) dado into the underside of the shelf, ⅞ inch (2.22 cm) from the front of the shelf. The dado should extend the full length of the shelf. This dado will receive the top edge of the front bottom

rail. The front corners of the bottom shelf are cut to fit around each of the posts.

Bevel the top front edge of the bottom shelf according to guidelines drawn ¼ inch (.64 cm) down from the top along the front edge and ¾ inch (1.91 cm) back from the front edge along the top. Cut the bevel with a block plane. Round the front two corners of the bottom shelf with a ¼-inch (.64-cm) radius template as a guide.

Subassembly

Bevel all through tenons with a disc sander or block plane. Use guidelines drawn ³⁄₁₆ inch (.47 cm) down from the end along each side and ⅛ inch (.32 cm) in from each edge on the end.

Also bevel the top of each post according to guidelines drawn ¼ inch (.64 cm) down from the top edge on each side and ¼ inch (.64 cm) in from all edges on the top.

Glue together each side unit, applying glue only to the mortise-and-tenon joints while allowing the panels free movement. This movement is necessary to prevent the panels from splitting or putting undue pressure on the frame if they expand.

When each side unit is dry, connect the two sides with the shelves, rails, and back panels to form the frame. Like the side panels, the back panels are left free.

Pin the tenons in the front bottom, the back, and the top side rails with ⅜-inch (.95-cm) dowels, centered on the post and tenon.

Door

Door Frame

Cut a ½-inch-wide (1.27-cm) by ½-inch-deep (1.27-cm) rabbet into

5-90. Cut a rabbet in the stile using a table saw. A support clamped to the table holds the stile against the fence as it passes over the blade.

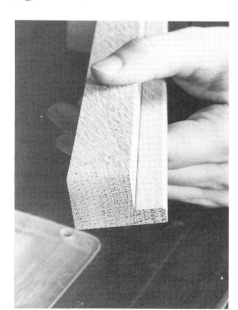

5-91. Finished rabbet cut in the stile.

the inside edges of the stiles and rails with a table saw. Use a support clamped to the table to hold the stock in place while you cut (figure 5-90). Cut a ¼-inch-wide (.64-cm) by ½-inch-deep (1.27-cm) rabbet in both edges of all mullions (figure 5-91).

Cut barefaced tenons measuring ¹³⁄₁₆ inch (2.06 cm) wide by ⁵⁄₁₆ inch (.79 cm) thick onto the ends of the top and bottom rails (figure 5-92). Set the dado blade of the table saw to cut ¼ inch (.64 cm) in depth. Clamp a stop on the miter guide to remove 1 inch (2.54 cm) of material from the end. Cut with the face of the rail resting on the table. Reset the dado blade of the table saw to cut ³⁄₁₆ inch (.47 cm) in depth and clamp a stop on the miter guide to remove ½ inch (1.27 cm) of material from the end. Cut with the back of the rail resting on the table. With the blade and miter guide stop in the same positions, place the face against the miter guide and make the final tenon cut.

Locate mortises on the inside edge of the stiles; draw the mortise ³⁄₁₆ inch (.47 cm) in from the end and ³⁄₁₆ inch (.47 cm) in from the back of the stile. Cut the mortise using the drill and chisel cleanout method (figure 5-93).

Mullions

Measure and mark the position of each lap joint on the horizontal mullions (figure 5-95). Cut a dado ½ inch (1.27 cm) wide and ¼ inch (.64 cm) deep into the body of the rabbet. Clamp a jig with a round bottom into position to prevent the stock from chattering on the saw.

Measure and mark the position of each lap joint on the vertical mullions (figure 5-95). First cut the wider, 1-inch (2.54-cm) dado into the face of the vertical mullions. Cut to a depth of ¼ inch

151

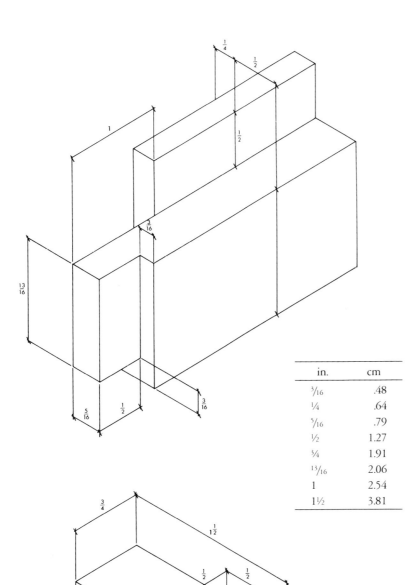

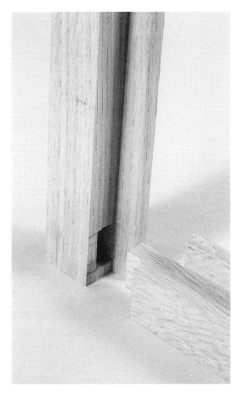

5-93. Cut a mortise in the stiles using drill and chisel cleanout method.

5-94. Finished barefaced mortise-and-tenon joint for door stile and rail.

in.	cm
³⁄₁₆	.48
¼	.64
⁵⁄₁₆	.79
½	1.27
¾	1.91
¹³⁄₁₆	2.06
1	2.54
1½	3.81

5-92. Working drawing for barefaced tenon.

in.	cm
¼	.64
½	1.27
¾	1.91
1	2.54

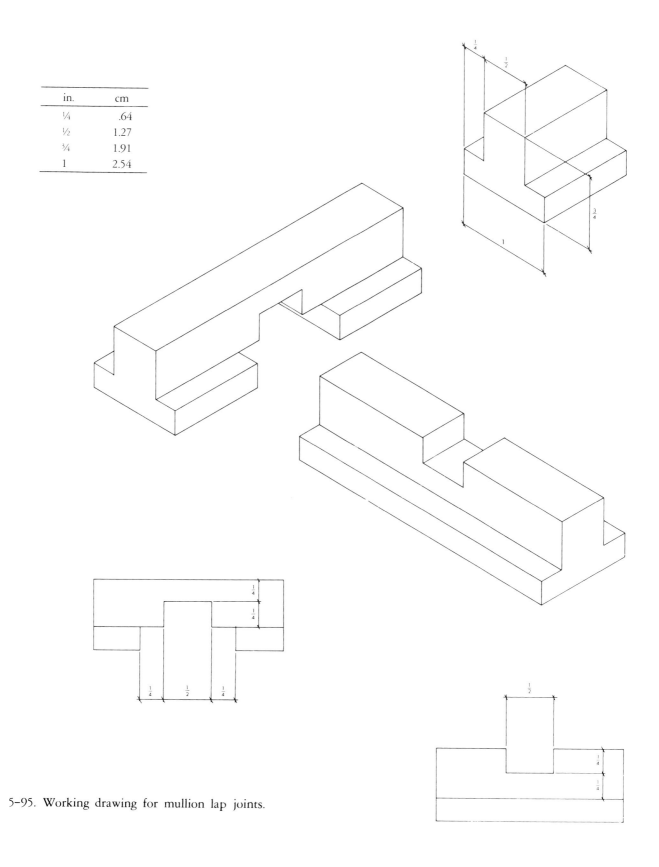

5-95. Working drawing for mullion lap joints.

(.64 cm), which should be exactly through the shoulders of the rabbet. You will have to make two passes to obtain the required width for the dado. Again, use a jig to prevent the stock from lifting. A second lap cut must be made to accommodate the rabbet bodies of the horizontal mullions. Set the table saw to cut to a depth of ½ inch (1.27 cm). Center this cut on the 1-inch (2.54-cm) dado.

Cut combination rabbet and mortise-and-tenon joints on the ends of the center vertical mullion and the horizontal mullion (figure 5-97). Set the dado blade of the

table saw to cut ¼ inch (.64 cm) depth and clamp a stop on the miter guide to remove 1 inch (2.54 cm) of material from the end. Cut with the face of the mullion resting on the table. With the blade of the table saw at the same depth and a stop on the miter guide set to remove ½ inch (1.27 cm) of material from the end, make a final cut with the back of the mullion resting on the table (figure 5-98). See chapter 4 for general instructions on cutting barefaced tenons.

Locate mortises on the inside edge of the stiles; draw the mor-

tises' center lines ⅜ inch (.95 cm) from the backs of the stiles, and the tops of the mortises 9⅞ inches (25.08 cm) from the tops of the stiles. Locate the mortises on the inside edge of the rails; draw the mortises' center lines ⅜ inch (.95 cm) from the back of the rail and the ends of the mortises 9⅞ inches (25.08 cm) from the end of the rail. Cut mortises using the drill and chisel cleanout method.

Cut a rabbet into the ends of the side vertical mullions where they will join the frame. Set the dado blade of the table saw to cut to a ¼-inch (.64-cm) depth, and clamp a stop on the miter guide to remove ½ inch (1.27 cm) of material from the top of each mullion. Cut with the face of the mullion resting on the table. Move the stop on the miter guide to remove ¼ inch (.64 cm) of material from the bottom of each mullion. Cut with the face of the mullion on the table.

Glue and clamp together the stiles, the top and bottom rails, and the center vertical and horizontal mullions. When this assembly is dry, glue and clamp the two side vertical mullions in place.

Assembly

Two pairs of stops are needed to properly align the doors. One pair, square in cross section, measures ½ inch (1.27 cm) wide by ½ inch (1.27 cm) thick by 2 inches (5.08 cm) long. The other pair, L-shaped in cross section, measures ½ inch (1.27 cm) wide by 1 inch (2.54 cm) thick by 42⅜ inches (107.63 cm) long (figure 5-99).

The L-shaped stops, also called hinge supports, are used to aid in mounting the box hinges for the doors to the case. They keep the hinge pin and its casing from rub-

5–96. Lap joint in center vertical and horizontal mullions.

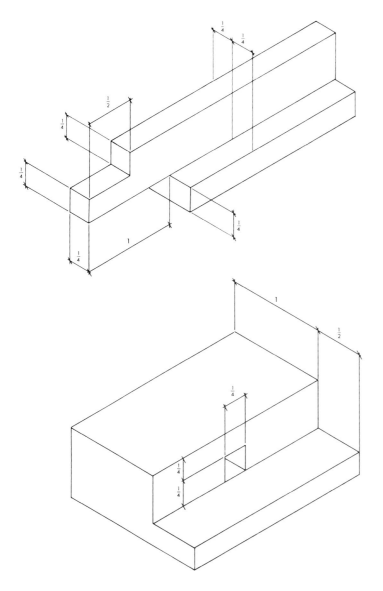

in.	cm
¼	.64
½	1.27
1	2.54

5-97. Working drawing for combination rabbet/mortise-and-tenon joint.

5-98. Combination rabbet/mortise-and-tenon joint connecting mullions to stiles and rails.

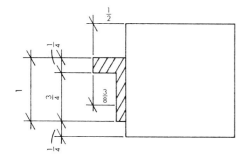

in.	cm
¼	.64
⅜	.95
½	1.27
¾	1.91
1	2.54

5-99. Working drawing for L-shaped stop.

in.	cm
¼	.64
⅜	.95
⅝	1.58
1	2.54
1⅛	2.86
1¼	3.17
4	10.16

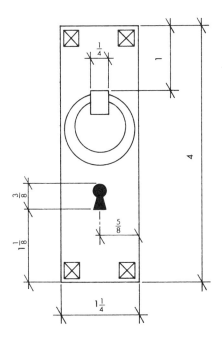

5-100. Working drawing for door-pull, front view.

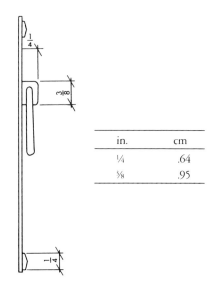

in.	cm
¼	.64
⅜	.95

5-101. Working drawing for door-pull, side view.

bing against the inside surface of the post. This is necessary because the door fronts are recessed from the front face of the posts. Glue the L-shaped stops with their 1 inch (2.54 cm) dimension against the post and their front edges ¼ inch (.64 cm) back from the front face of the post along the inside edge of the post between the top and bottom shelves.

Apply a finish to the piece using the procedure described in chapter 4.

Use four 3-inch (7.62-cm) loose pin brass box hinges to attach the doors to the case. Treat the surfaces of the hinges according to the instructions given in chapter 4. Position the top hinge on each door so that the top of the hinge is 4 inches (10.16 cm) down from the underside of the top shelf. Position the bottom of the lower hinge 4 inches (10.16 cm) up from the top surface of the bottom shelf.

Cut hinge-plate mortises using the instructions given in chapter 4. Then connect hinges and doors to the case.

The square stops will prevent the doors from closing too far into the case. Close both doors and hold a long, steel straightedge horizontally against their front faces, making sure it makes contact along its full length with the door faces. Mark the bottom and top shelves by running a pencil along the inside of both doors where they meet. This line gives you the position of the forwardmost edge of the square stops. Glue both stops in place with their front edges along this line, centered on each shelf.

Drawings of the door-pull (figures 5-100 and 5-101) have been included so that you can make the pull or have it made by a

metalsmith. The pulls are made of solid copper; the plate, from 14-gauge (.625-inch [.16-cm]) sheet stock; the drop ring, from ¼-inch (.64-cm) rod stock; the pyramid shaped caps (which are soldered to the heads of brass wood screws) from 8-gauge (.128-inch [.32-cm]) sheet stock; and the drop ring pivot block from ¼-inch (.64-cm) by ⅜-inch (.95-cm) bar stock. The plate is planished, and forging marks are left in the drop ring. See figure 5-89 for location of pulls on the doors.

The left door is held closed by a spring-action elbow latch attached to the inside of the door and the underside of the center shelf. This latch should be installed according to the instructions provided by the manufacturer. The right door is held closed with a small mortise cupboard lock. The bolt of this lock enters a mortise in the edge of the left door. Position the lock so that its keyhole is in line with the keyhole cut in the door pull. This lock mechanism can be purchased at most hardware stores and should be installed according to the manufacturer's instructions.

To install the glass, remove the pins from the hinges and take off the doors. Measure each opening in the back side of the door for glass size. Cut or have the glass cut so that it fits each opening with 1/16 inch (.15 cm) of play. To hold the glass in position, nail ¼ inch (.64 cm) wide by ⅜ inch (.95 cm) thick molding strips in place with small brads.

Additional shelves can be made as desired for the areas above and below the middle shelf. These adjustable shelves can be supported by dowel pins inserted in the holes or by shelf brackets, which can be purchased in most hardware stores.

Clock Case

This hall clock case, as Stickley named it, exemplifies the structural style applied to a traditional furniture piece. The clock case retains the formality of a grandfather clock, but Stickley redefined the usual ornamentation in terms of the functional mullions on the door. A rather detailed design for a Craftsman piece, the elements nonetheless remain functional.

157

MATERIALS

	Number of Pieces	Length in.	Length cm	Width in.	Width cm	Thickness in.	Thickness cm
Frame							
Side	2	71¼	180.98	10	25.40	1¼	3.17
Top Shelf	1	20½	52.07	10¾	27.31	1¼	3.17
Bottom Shelf	1	16¾	42.55	8¼	20.96	⅞	2.22
Front and Back Bottom Rail	2	19	48.26	4	10.16	⅞	2.22
Top Back Rail	1	17	43.18	5⅞	14.92	⅞	2.22
Back Panel	1	47⅛	119.70	17	43.18	½	1.27
Movement Shelf	1	17	43.18	5	12.70	⅞	2.22
Back Door							
Top and Bottom Back-Door Rail	2	16	40.64	2½	6.35	⅞	2.22
Side Back-Door Rail	2	9	22.86	2½	6.35	⅞	2.22
Back-Door Panel	1	12	30.48	10	25.40	½	1.27
Front Door							
Door Stile	2	66	167.64	1⅞	4.76	¾	1.91
Top and Middle Door Rail	2	13⅞	35.24	2	5.08	¾	1.91
Bottom Door Rail	1	13⅞	35.24	3	7.62	¾	1.91
Vertical Door Mullion	3	48⅞	124.14	1	2.54	¾	1.91
Horizontal Door Mullion	11	13⅞	35.24	1	2.54	¾	1.91
Stops							
Front Stop	1	66	167.64	½	1.27	½	1.27
Front Hinge Support	1	66	167.64	1⅛	2.86	⅝	1.58
Back Stop	1	14	35.56	½	1.27	½	1.27
Back Hinge Support	1	14	35.56	1⅛	2.86	⅝	1.58
Glass							
Corner Panes	4	3¹¹⁄₁₆	9.37	2¹⁵⁄₁₆	7.46	⅛	.32
Side Panes	20	3⁷⁄₁₆	8.73	2¹⁵⁄₁₆	7.46	⅛	.32
Center Top and Bottom Panes	4	3¹¹⁄₁₆	9.37	2¹¹⁄₁₆	6.83	⅛	.32
Center Panes	20	3⁷⁄₁₆	8.73	2¹¹⁄₁₆	6.83	⅛	.32
Clock-Face Pane	1	12¹⁵⁄₁₆	32.86	12¹⁵⁄₁₆	32.86	⅛	.32

⅜-inch (.95-cm) dowels
⅝-inch (1.58-cm) dowels
3 loose-pin brass or steel box hinges, 3 inches (7.62 cm) long
2 loose-pin brass or steel box hinges, 1½ inches (3.81 cm) long
1 small mortise cupboard lock
molding strips: for lower door, 1 strip, 52 feet (15.86 m) by ¼ inch (.64 cm) by ⅜ inch (.95 cm); for clock face, 1 strip, 5 feet (1.52 m) by ½ inch (1.27 cm) by ⅜ inch (.95 cm)
brads

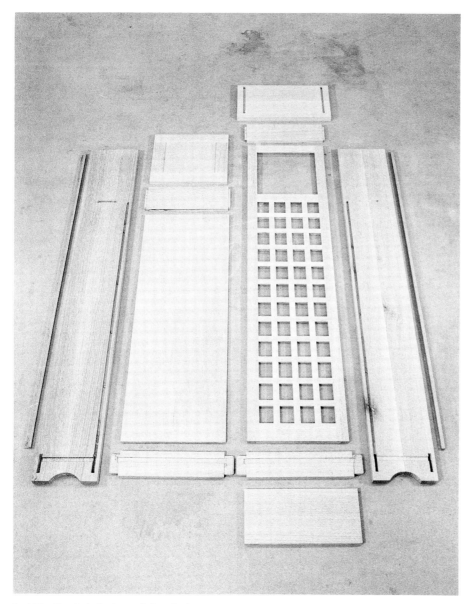

5-103. Exploded view of the clock case.

5-104. Clock case.

This clock case has three subassemblies: the frame, the back door, and the front door. The frame, which is constructed first, consists of two sides, a top and bottom shelf, a front and back bottom rail, a top back rail, a back panel, and a movement shelf that will hold the clock. The back door, a simple frame construction, is made from a top and bottom rail, two side rails, and a back-door panel. The most difficult of the subassemblies, the front door is built with two stiles, a top, middle, and bottom rail, three vertical mullions, and eleven horizontal mullions. Cut your stock according to the dimensions given in the materials list.

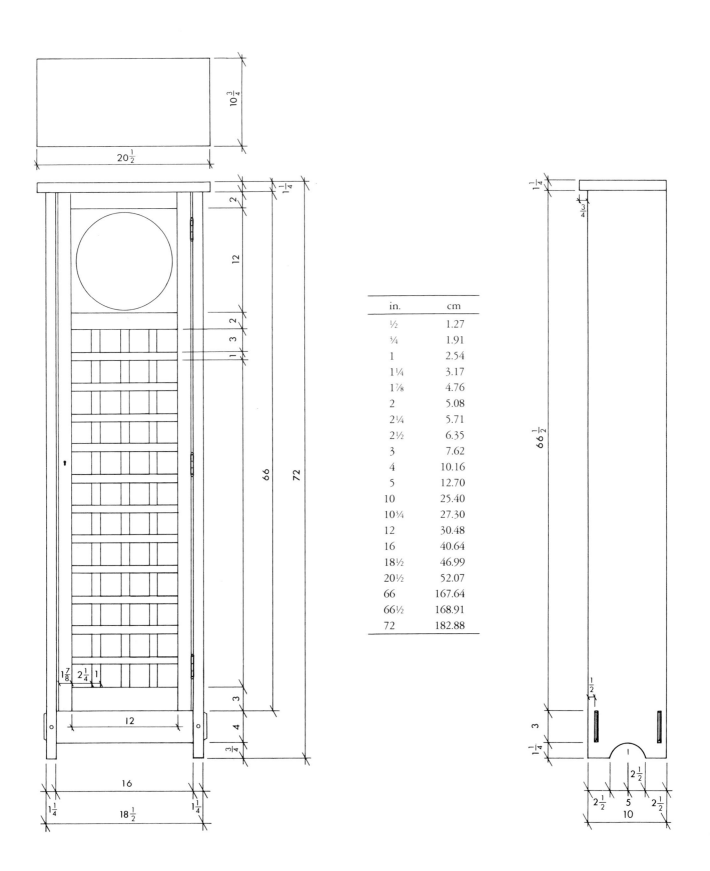

in.	cm
½	1.27
¾	1.91
1	2.54
1¼	3.17
1⅞	4.76
2	5.08
2¼	5.71
2½	6.35
3	7.62
4	10.16
5	12.70
10	25.40
10¾	27.30
12	30.48
16	40.64
18½	46.99
20½	52.07
66	167.64
66½	168.91
72	182.88

5-105. Working drawing for clock case. Front and side views.

PROCEDURE

In addition to the instructions given below, you may need to refer to the general instructions in chapter 4 for the following procedures:

Butt-joining, page 71
Squaring laminated stock, pages 74–75
Cutting tenons, pages 65–66
Cutting mortises with router, pages 76–77
Cutting mortises with drill and chisel, page 69
Beveling, page 70
Assembly, pages 79–83
Treating hinges, page 88
Cutting hinge mortises, page 88
Finishing, pages 84–87

Frame

Laminate the sides, the top shelf, and the bottom shelf by joining two boards edge-to-edge with ⅝-inch (1.58-cm) dowels. Lay out each part carefully, alternating the end grain direction of the boards to minimize warping.

Trim one end of each laminated piece square with a router. Measure the pieces to length and trim the other end.

Cut a blind tenon measuring 9 inches (22.86 cm) wide by ½ inch (1.27 cm) long by ⅝-inch (1.58-cm) thick on the top end of each side (figure 5-107). Using a router and a ⅝-inch (1.58-cm) straight bit with a fence or guide, make a cut ⁵⁄₁₆ inch (.79 cm) in depth from each face. This will give you the ⅝-inch (1.58-cm) thickness and ½-inch (1.27-cm) length of the tenon. (Make your router cut in several passes.) To establish the width, cut in from each edge ½ inch (1.27 cm) in depth with a backsaw. To finish the tenon,

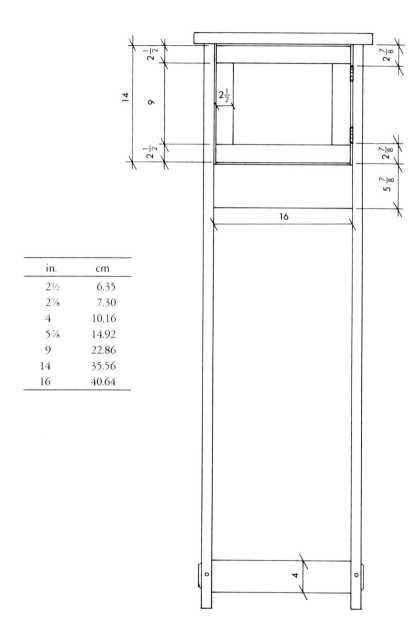

in.	cm
2½	6.35
2⅞	7.30
4	10.16
5⅞	14.92
9	22.86
14	35.56
16	40.64

5-106. Working drawing for clock case. Back view.

slowly chip away material with a flat chisel, on the end grain and moving toward the saw mark. Make several cuts, each taking off more material, until you approach the end of the saw cut. Make your last cut at a ninety-degree angle to the saw cut.

Cut mortises for these tenons in the underside of the top shelf with a router and a ⅝-inch (1.58-cm) straight bit. Locate the center of each mortise 1¼ inches (3.17 cm) in from the side edge, beginning ½ inch (1.27 cm) from the back edge (figure 5-107).

Cut through tenons measuring 3 inches (7.62 cm) wide by 1½ inches (3.81 cm) long by ½ inch (1.27 cm) thick on both ends of the front and back bottom rails. Locate their mortises in the sides (figure 5-105) and cut, using the drill and chisel cleanout method.

Bevel the ends of the through tenons with a disc sander or block plane. Cut the bevel according to guidelines drawn ³⁄₁₆ inches (.47 cm) down from the end along each side and ⅛ inch (.32 cm) in from each edge on the end.

Using a table saw with a ⅞-inch (2.22-cm) dado blade, cut a dado ⅞ inch (2.22 cm) wide by ⅜ inch (.95 cm) deep into the inside faces of the front and back bottom rails. The top edge of each dado should begin 1 inch (2.54 cm) down from the top edge of each rail. Cut only shoulder to shoulder on each rail; chisel out the remainder of the dado so that the full bottom shelf seats properly (figure 5-108).

Dry-clamp both bottom rails into their mortises. With a pencil, locate where each dado intersects the sides of the clock case. Remove the rails and connect the intersection marks mortise to mortise. This gives you the position of the bottom shelf dado. Cut a dado

⅞ inch (2.22 cm) wide by ⅜ inch (.95 cm) deep on each side, using a router with a ⅝-inch (1.58-cm)

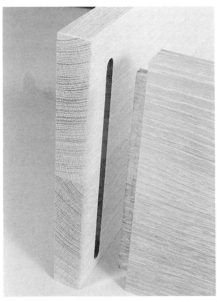

5-107. Mortise and tenon join side and top shelf of clock case.

straight bit along a fence or guide. Two passes with the ⅝-inch (1.58-cm) bit, moving the fence or guide between passes, are necessary to cut a ⅞-inch-wide (2.22-cm) dado.

Cut blind tenons, measuring 4⅞ inches (12.38 cm) wide by ½ inch (1.27 cm) long by ½ inch (1.27 cm) thick on both ends of the top back rail. Locate and cut mortises on inner clock sides using the router with a ½-inch (1.27-cm) straight bit and a fence or guide. Cut these mortises the same distance from the back edge of the sides as the mortises for the back bottom rail.

Cut ½-inch-wide (1.27-cm) by ½-inch-deep (1.27-cm) dados, on center into the top edge of the back bottom rail and the bottom edge of the top back rail, using the

5-108. Dados cut in bottom rails hold bottom shelf.

5–109. Back-door frame, showing panel in place and doweled butt joint in corners.

router and a ½-inch (1.27-cm) straight bit. These dados will accommodate the back panel.

Using the router with a ½-inch (1.27-cm) straight bit and a fence or guide, cut a ½-inch-deep (1.27-cm) dado into each side for insertion of the back panel. This dado should connect the mortises of the top and bottom back rails.

Cut blind tenons measuring 4½ inches (11.43 cm) wide by ½ inch (1.27 cm) long by ½ inch (1.27 cm) thick in the ends of the movement shelf. Locate its mortises 14 ⅜ inches (36.51 cm) on

center, from the underside of the top shelf. Cut the mortises with a router and a ½-inch (1.27-cm) straight bit.

Using a saber saw, cut the arc in the bottom of each side to the dimensions given in figure 5-108. Finish the arc with a file and sandpaper.

The frame of the clock case is now ready for subassembly. Apply glue only to the mortise-and-tenon joints; leave the back panel free to prevent it from splitting or putting undue pressure on the frame if it expands.

Back Door

The back door is a simple frame construction held together with butt joints and ⅜-inch (.95-cm) dowels (figure 5-109). After making the butt joints, cut a ½-inch-wide (1.27-cm) dado ½ inch (1.27 cm) deep, on center, into the inside edges of all four door rails with the router table and a ½-inch (1.27-cm) straight bit. Round the corners of the back-door panel for ease in assembly. To assemble the back door, apply glue only to the butt joints, leaving the back-door panel free.

163

Front Door

Door Frame

Cut a rabbet ½ inch (1.27 cm) deep by ½ inch (1.27 cm) wide into the inside edge of each stile and rail (both edges of the middle rail).

Cut barefaced tenons measuring 1¹⁄₁₆ inch (2.7 cm) wide by ⁵⁄₁₆ inch (.79 cm) thick onto both ends of the top and bottom rails (figure 5-110). Set the dado blade of a table saw to cut ¼ inch (.64 cm) in depth. Clamp a stop on the miter guide to remove 1 inch (2.54 cm) of material from the end. Cut with the face of the rail resting on the table. Reset the dado blade of the table saw to cut ³⁄₁₆ inch (.47 cm) in depth and clamp a stop on the miter guide to remove ½ inch (1.27 cm) of material from the end. Cut with the back of the rail resting on the table. With the blade and miter guide stop in the same positions, place the face against the miter guide and make the final tenon cut.

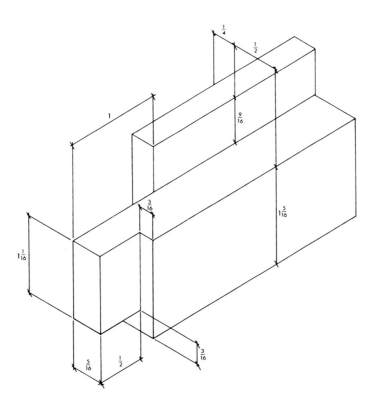

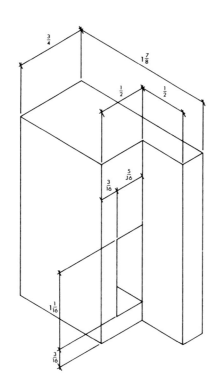

5-110. Working drawing of barefaced tenon.

in.	cm
³⁄₁₆	.48
¼	.64
⁵⁄₁₆	.79
½	1.27
⁹⁄₁₆	1.43
¾	1.91
1	2.54
1¹⁄₁₆	2.70
1⁵⁄₁₆	3.33
1⁷⁄₈	4.76

Cut the mortises in the stiles using the drill and chisel cleanout method (see figure 5-105 for location).

Cut a rabbet joint and then a tenon on the middle rail (figure 5-111). Set the dado blade of the table saw to cut ¼ inch (.64 cm) in depth. Clamp a stop on the miter guide to remove 1 inch (2.54 cm) of material from the end. Cut with the face of the rail resting on the table. With the blade of the table saw at the same depth and a stop on the miter guide to remove ½ inch (1.27 cm) of material from the end, make the final cut with the back of the rail resting on the table.

Locate the position of the rail mortises on the stiles and cut, using the same procedure as for the top and bottom rails.

Glue and assemble the door frame.

in.	cm
¼	.64
½	1.27
1	2.54

5–111. Working drawing for combination rabbet/mortise-and-tenon joint.

Mullions

Cut a rabbet on two sides of each mullion ½ inch (1.27 cm) deep by ¼ inch (.64 cm) wide (figures 5-112 and 5-113). Measure and mark the position of each lap joint on the horizontal mullions (see figures 5-105 and 5-114) To cut the lap joints in the horizontal mullions, cut a dado ½ inch (1.27 cm) wide and ¼ inch (.64 cm) deep into the body of the rabbet (figure 5-115). Clamp a jig with a round bottom into position to prevent the stock from chattering on the saw. Use a stop on the end of the stock to aid in positioning the cuts equidistant from each end. Cut all lap joints on horizontal mullions this way.

With the jig in place, line the stock up with the dado blade to cut the center lap. Reposition the stop at the end of the stock and cut all center laps on all horizontal mullions.

Measure and mark the position of each lap joint on the three vertical mullions (figure 5-114). First cut the wider, 1-inch (2.54-cm) dado into the face of the vertical mullions. Cut to a depth of ¼ inch (.64 cm), which should be exactly through the shoulders of the rabbet. You will have to make two passes to obtain the required width for the dado. Again, use a jig to prevent the stock from lifting. After cutting the first dado in each mullion, insert a stop into the shoulder of the first cut and clamp it at the appropriate distance from the blade to align the second cut. This will serve as a guide for the remaining cuts as the stock is moved along (figure 5-116).

5–113. Finished mullion, showing rabbet cut in both edges.

5–112. Cut a rabbet in a mullion with a table saw. A support clamped to the table holds the mullion against the fence as it passes over the blade.

166

in.	cm
¼	.64
½	1.27
¾	1.91
1	2.54

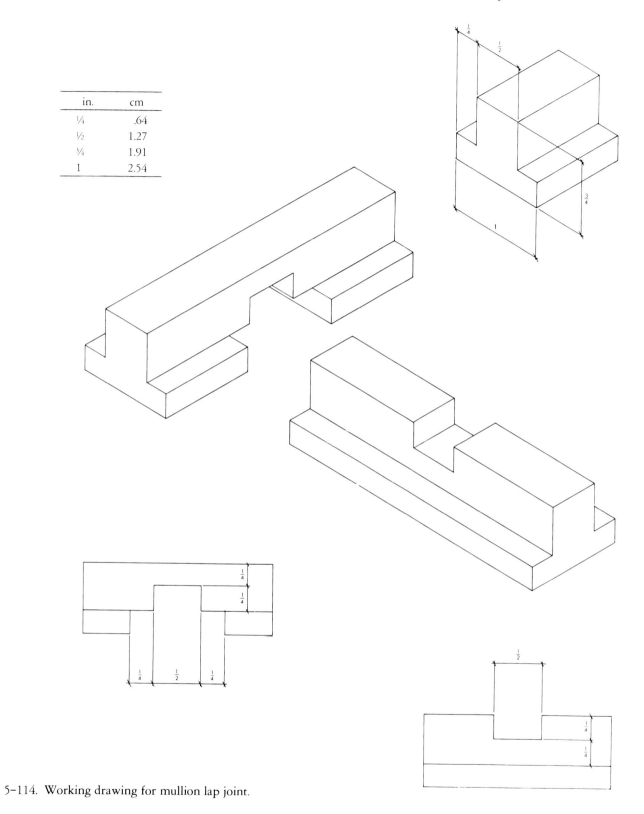

5-114. Working drawing for mullion lap joint.

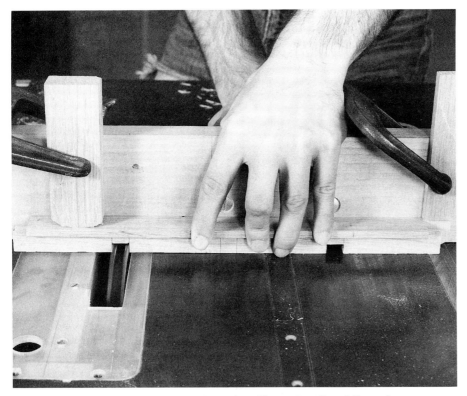

5-115. Cutting lap joints in the horizontal mullions. A radiused jig and a stop are clamped to the miter guide.

5-116. Cutting the second lap joint on a vertical mullion, radiused jig and stop in place.

When all of the 1-inch-wide (2.54-cm) dados have been cut in the vertical mullions, a second lap cut must be made to accommodate the rabbet bodies of the horizontal mullions. Center these cuts on the 1-inch (2.54-cm) dados. Using the same stop, make your first lap cut. Move the stock into position for the second cut and clamp the stop into position, touching the inside shoulder of the first dado cut. Proceed to make all lap cuts on each vertical mullion.

Cut a rabbet into the face of each end of all mullions where they will join the frame. Make these rabbets ¼ inch (.64 cm) deep and ½ inch (1.27 cm) back from the end.

Assembly

Because so many joints must be assembled, you should glue the horizontal mullions to the vertical mullions three at a time. Tape unglued mullions in place to maintain proper alignment as you proceed. When all mullions have been glued, try the resulting mullion assembly in the door frame and make any adjustments to assure a perfect fit. With adjustments completed, glue the mullion subassembly into the door frame.

The front and back stops will prevent the front and back doors from closing too far into the case. A second pair of stops, one for each door, also serves as a hinge support. These stops will require a rabbet cut, as illustrated in figure 5-117.

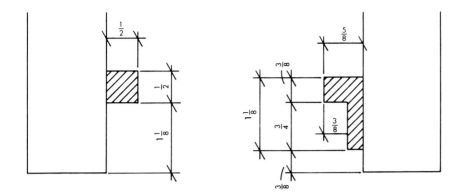

5-117. Working drawing for hinge supports and stops.

in.	cm
⅜	.95
½	1.27
⅝	1.58
¾	1.91
1⅛	2.86

Glue the front stop to the left front side of the clock case, with its front face set back 1⅛ inch (2.86 cm) from the front edge of the side of the frame (figure 5-118). Glue the front hinge support to the right front side, its front face set back ⅜ inch (.95 cm) from the front edge of the side of the frame.

Glue the back stop to the left backside of the frame, with its front face 1¼ inches (3.17 cm) from the back edge of the frame. Glue the back hinge support to the right back side, set back ½ inch (1.27 cm) from the back edge of the frame. Apply a finish to the piece.

Next, locate the position of the hinges for the doors. The back door uses two 1½-inch (3.81-cm) brass loose-pin hinges. Locate the top of the upper hinge 2⅞ inches (7.30 cm) down from the underside of the top shelf. Position the bottom of the lower hinge 2⅞ inches (7.30 cm) up from the top edge of the top back rail (figure 5-119).

5-118. Door stop clamped in position with the aid of pine alignment blocks. Alignment block should be dry-clamped to the clock side before door stop is glued and clamped in place.

The front door uses three 3-inch (7.62-cm) brass loose-pin hinges. Locate the top of the upper hinge 4 ½ inches (11.43 cm) from the underside of the top shelf. Position the bottom of the lower hinge 4½ inches (11.43 cm) up from the top edge of the bottom rail. Locate the top of the center hinge 31½ inches (80.01 cm) down from the underside of the top shelf.

Treat the hinge surfaces according to the instructions given in chapter 4. Then connect the hinges and doors to the clock.

The final step is to install the locking mechanism opposite the center hinge, centered on the left door stile. The lock is a small mortise cupboard lock, the bolt of which enters a mortise in the left clock side. This lock mechanism can be purchased at most hardware stores and should be installed according to the manufacturers instructions.

To install the glass, remove the pins from the hinges and take off the door. Measure each opening in the back side of the door for glass size. Cut or have the glass cut to fit each opening, allowing $\frac{1}{16}$-inch (.15-cm) of play. To hold the glass in position in the lower door, nail ½-inch-wide (.64-cm) by ⅜-inch-thick (.95-cm) molding strips in place with small brads. Do the same for the clock-face glass, but instead use ½-inch (1.27-cm) by ½-inch (1.27-cm) molding strips.

The clock itself can be chosen from any supplier but should meet several requirements. It should be a pendulum movement driven by weights. The maximum pendulum swing should be less than 16 inches (40.64 cm).

The face of the clock can be made of wood or metal. If you choose wood, it should be a fine-grained species, such as holly or orange, with numbers burned in or inlaid with pewter. If you decide on a metal face, it should be made of copper with pewter numbers. We also suggest that the numbers chosen for any face be from an old-style typeface.

5–119. Finished back door of the clock.

Bibliography

BOOKS

Andrews, Edward and Faith. *Shaker Furniture*: The Craftsmanship of an American Communal Sect. 1937. Reprint. New York: Dover Publications, 1964.

Bossaglia, Rossana. *Revolution in Interior Design*. London: Orbis Connoisseurs, 1973.

Champigneulle, Bernard. *Art Noveau*. Woodbury, New York: Barrons Educational Series, 1976.

Charlish, Anne, ed. *The History of Furniture*. New York: William Morrow and Company, 1976.

Clark, Robert Judson, ed. *The Arts and Crafts Movement in America*. Princeton, New Jersey. Princeton University Press, 1972.

Cobden-Sanderson, T. J. *The Arts and Crafts Movement*. Hammersmith Publishing Society, 1905.

Feirer, John L., and Hutchings, Gilbert R. *Advanced Woodwork and Furniture-Making*. 4th ed. Peoria, Illinois: Chas. A. Bennett Company, 1972.

Franco, Borsi, and Egio, Goduli. *Paris 1900*. New York: Rizzoli, 1977.

Freeman, John Crosby. *The Forgotten Rebel*. Watkins Glen, New York: Century House Publishing, 1966.

Handlin, Oscar, ed. *Readings in American History*. New York: Alfred A. Knopf, 1957.

Hayes, Carlton J. H. *Contemporary Europe Since 1870*. New York: The Macmillan Company, 1958.

Joyce, Ernest. *Encyclopedia of Furniture Making*. New York: Sterling Publishing Company, 1979.

Kane, Patricia E. *Three Hundred Years of American Seating Furniture*. Toronto, Canada: Little, Brown and Company, New York Graphic Society Books, 1976.

Leonard, John W., ed. "Stickley, Gustav." In *Who's Who in America, 1906-07*. Chicago: A.N. Marquis Company, 1907.

Rheims, Maurice. *The Flowering of Art Nouveau*. New York: Harry N. Abrams, 1966.

Schmutzler, Robert. *Art Nouveau*. New York: Harry N. Abrams, 1978.

Smelser, Marshall. *American History at a Glance*. New York: Harper and Row Publishers, Barnes and Noble Books, 1971.

Stickley, Gustav. *Craftsman Homes:* Architecture and Furnishings of the American Arts and Crafts Movement. New York: Dover Publications, Reprint. 1979.

Stickley, Gustav. *More Craftsman Homes*. New York: Craftsman Publishing Company, 1913.

Talmon, J. R. *Romanticism and Revolt: Europe 1815-1848*. New York: W. W. Norton and Company, 1979.

Thompson, Paul. *The Work of William Morris*. New York: Quartet Books, 1977.

PERIODICALS

Gilbert, Charles B. "Manual Training in Public Schools." *Manual Training Magazine*, April, 1902, p. 129.

Koch, Robert. "Will Bradley." *Art in America*, Fall, 1962, pps. 78-83.

Priestman, Mabel Tukc. "History of the Arts and Crafts Movement in America." *The House Beautiful*, September, 1904, pps. 15-16.

Stickley, Gustav. *Chips from the Workshops of Gustav Stickley*. (2 issues.) New York, 1907.

Stickley, Gustav. *The Craftsman*. October, 1901-December, 1916.

Stickley, Gustav. "The Structural Style in Cabinet Making." *The House Beautiful*, December, 1903, pps. 20-25.

Index

A

Adjustable band screws, 79
Advertising, art nouveau and, 9
Air-drying of lumber, 62
Aliphatic resin glue, 82
Alliance Française, 22
"Als ik kan," 20
Aluminum oxide paper, 78–79
American Museum of Natural
    History, 60
Ammonia. *See* Fuming
Architecture and houses, 15–16, 22,
    23, 24, 29, 38
    plan for Craftsman Farms, 26
    Stickley on use of wood in, 60
Arm chair, 42
Arm rocker, 39
Art nouveau, 9
    at Arts and Crafts Exhibition,
        22–23
    Stickley and, 19
Art pottery, 14–15, 19–20
Arts and Crafts Exhibition (1903),
    22–23
Arts and Crafts furniture (specific
    manufactured style), 26
Arts and Crafts movement, 9–16, 35
Ashbee (Arts and Crafts master), 19
Assembly, 79–83. *See also* specific
    projects
    clamps, 79–80
    cleaning up, 81–82
    dowel-pinning mortise and tenon,
        82–83
    dry-clamping, 80
    glides, 82
    glue selection and procedure, 80–81
Atterbury, Grosvenor, 25

B

Auburn, NY, 18
Auburn Prison, 18

Band clamp, 79
Barefaced tenon, 67–68. *See also*
    Projects
Beaux arts, 8–9
Beds, 33
Bending of wood, 77–78
Bent stock, cutting tenons on, 66–67.
    See also Projects
Beveling, 70
Bing, Samuel, 19, 29
Binghamton, NY, 17–18
Binghamton Street Railway, 18
Board feet, determining, 62
Boiling water, for bending of wood,
    77–78
Bookcase (project), 143–56
    combination bookcase and table
        (project), 100–6
Borders, art nouveau, 9
Bows (bowed lumber), 63, 64
Bradley, Will H., 9
Brandt, Schuyler C., 17
Brandt, PA, 17
Brandt Chair Company, 17
Brass hinges, 88
British, the. *See* England and the
    British
Bronze hinges, 88
Brown, Ford Madox, 10
Buffalo, NY, 19
Burne-Jones, Edward, 10, 11
Butterfly joints, 98–99
Butt joints, 71

C

Cabinet clamp, 79
Carlyle, Thomas, 17
Case-hardening, 62
Cathedrals, Gothic, 34
C-clamp, 79
Ceramics. *See* Pottery
Chairs,
    bending wood for, 77–78
    from catalog, 39, 40, 41, 42, 43
    recliner (project), 117–28
    rocker (project), 108–16
    seat frames and upholstery, 88
Checks and checking (checked
    lumber), 61, 63, 64
    filling, 78
Cherry Valley furniture, 31
Chestnut, 61
    fuming, 84
Child's table, 49
China cabinet, 51
Chinese Chippendale furniture, 31
Chromewald furniture, 31
Clamps, 79–80
    dry-clamping, 80
Clock case (project), 157–70
Color. *See* Finishing
Combination bookcase and table
    (project), 100–6
Copper-plating, 88
Costumer, 58
Craftsman, The (magazine), 16, 23,
    24–25, 26–29, 37, 89
    article on seat frames and
        upholstery, 88
    bookcase project from, 143–50
    eulogy for Harvey Ellis, 23–24
    founding of, first issues, 21–22

Grueby pottery shown in, 20
last issue, 31
moves to New York, 24
Craftsman, The, Inc., 29–31
Craftsman Building (New York City), 30–31
Craftsman Building (Syracuse), 22–23
Craftsman Contracting Company, 29
Craftsman Farms, 26
food for restaurant grown at, 31
school for boys at, 29
sold, 31
Craftsman Homebuilder's Club, 24, 29
Craftsman Workshops, 25
Crafts-Style furniture, 26
Criminals, 29, 37–38
Crouse, Edgar, 22
Crouse Hall, 22
Crouse Stables, 22
Cups (cupped lumber), 63, 64
Cutting of wood. *See also* Joinery; Sawing
routers and, 75–77

D

Decoration,
art nouveau borders, 9
ornamentation and structural necessity, 34
Dents, removing, 79
Desk, 55, 56
Desk lamp, 57
Dining table (project), 136–47
Door pulls, 88, 158
Dowels, 70–71
and butt joints, 71
pinning mortise and tenon, 82–83
Dry-clamping, 80
Drying of woods, 62

E

East Aurora, NY, 14
Eastwood, NY, 19, 31, 32
Edge-bent lumber. *See* Springs
Education and schools, 29, 37
Ellis, Harvey, 23–24
Emerson, Ralph Waldo, 34
Engineer's Club, 26
England and the British, 9, 10–17
Stickley's visit, 19
Environment, 15–16. *See also* Architecture and houses
Epoxy resin glue, 78

Erotic imagery, beaux arts and, 9
Europe, 8*ff*., 33. *See also* England and the British; France
Stickley's visits, 19, 33
Eyck, Ian (Jan) van, 20

F

Farney family, 31
FAS (firsts and seconds), 62
Fayetteville, NY, 19, 31
Finishing, 37, 84–87
Stickley's notes on, 84–85
Fixed head bar clamp, 79
Flakes, 61–62
Flint paper, 78
Flying buttress, 34
Folding screen (project), 93–95
Footrest, 45
France, 9
and beds, 33
Stickley in, 19, 33
Fulper Pottery Company, 14
Fuming, 84–87
tent for, 85*ff*.
testing for color, 85–86
Furniture clamp, 79
Furniture World, 31

G

Garnet paper, 78
Gill, Irving, 25, 37
Glides, adding, 82
Glue, 80–81
cleaning up, 81–82
epoxy resin, 78
Gothic cathedrals, 34
Grading of wood, 62–63
Grand Rapids, MI, 17
Chromewald furniture at exhibition, 31
structural furniture exhibited, 19
Greene, Charles and Henry, 15–16, 25
"Green" wood, 62
Grueby, William H., 19
Grueby Faience and Tile Company, 14, 19–20
Guild of St. George, 10

H

Hall mirror, 58
Hand-Craft furniture, 26
Hardware, 87–88. *See also* specific projects

Hardwood. *See* Wood
Heartwood, 60
Hide glue, 80
Hinges, 88. *See also* specific projects
Hinge supports, 154–56
House Beautiful, The, 19, 23
Houses. *See* Architecture and houses
Hubbard, Elbert, 14
Hunt, Myron, 37
Hunt, William Holman, 10

I

Ironing of dents, 78

J

Japanese art, 22
Joinery (joints), 34, 65–71. *See also* Assembly; specific projects
beveling, 70
butt joints, 71
clamps and clamping, 79–80
dowels and dowel-pinning, 70–71, 82–83
mortise layout and cutting, 69–70
tenon layout and cutting, 65–68

K

Kelmscott Press, 12, 14, 21
Kenosha, WI, 31
Knots, 64
filling, 78

L

Lacquer and lacquering, 78, 84, 85
Lake Skaneateles, NY, 32
Lalique, René, 19
Legs. *See also* specific articles of furniture
glides for, 82
veneers for, 72–73
Lethaby, William Richard, 19
Library table, 48, 54
Limbert's Holland Dutch Arts and Crafts, 26
Lunch table, 49
Lusitania, S. S., 14

M

Machinery, 12, 35
Magazine cabinet, 50
Mahogany, 61
Maison l'art nouveau (Bing's shop), 19, 23

Marblehead Pottery, 14–15
Mark, Stickley's, 20–21
Measuring, in determining board feet, 62
Medullary rays, 61
Metal hardware, 87–88. *See also* specific projects
Middle class, Arts and Crafts and the, 10
Millais, John E., 10
Mirror,
    from catalog, 58
    project, 90–92
Morris, William, 9, 10–12, 15, 21, 117
    Craftsman dedication to, 21
    Kelmscott Press, 12, 14, 21
    Stickley becomes interested in, 17
    Stickley motto adopted from 20
Morris Plains, NJ, 26–29
Mortise-and-tenon joints, 34, 65–71.
    See also Projects
    beveling, 70
    dowels and dowel-pinning, 70–71, 82–83
    mortise layout and cutting, 69–70
    tenon layout and cutting, 65–68
Mortises. *See also* Mortise-and-tenon joints
    for hinges, 88
    router table and, 76–77
Motto, Stickley's, 20–21

N

National Arts Club, 26
New York City, 24, 29–31
    American Museum of Natural History, 60
New York Athletic Club, 26
#1 Common lumber, 62
#2 Common lumber, 62

O

Oak, 35–37
    drying of quarter-sawn, 62
    fumed, 84
    hardware for, 87–88
    sawing of, 61
Oakland, CA, 13–14
Oriental influences, 15, 22, 23
Ornament, and structural necessity, 34
Osceola, WI, 17

P

Pan-American Exposition, 19
Paris. *See also* France
    Exhibition (1900), 33
Patterns, 64. *See also* specific projects
Philadelphia Exhibition (1876), 8, 18
Piano lamp, 57
Pine, 61
    Southern, 60
Pipe clamp, 79
Plain-sawn wood, 61, 62
Posters, art nouveau and, 9
Pottery, 14–15, 19–20
Pre-Raphaelite brotherhood, 10
Projects, 89–170
    bookcase, 143–56
    clock case, 157–70
    combination bookcase and table, 100–6
    dining table, 136–42
    mirror, 90–92
    recliner, 117–28
    rocker, 108–16
    screen, 93–100
    settle, 129–35

Q

Quaint furniture (manufactured style), 26
Quarter-sawing, 61, 62

R

Ray flakes, 61, 62
Recliner,
    from catalog, 43
    project, 117–28
Red House, 11
Reproductions, Stickley and, 33
Revere (Paul) Pottery, 14
Ring flakes, 61, 62
Rockers,
    bending, 77–78
    from catalog, 39, 40
    project, 108–16
Rodin, Auguste, 37
Rookwood Pottery, 14
Roosevelt, Theodore, 37
Rossetti, Dante Gabriel, 10, 11
Routers, 74–77
Roycrofters, 14
Ruskin, John, 9, 10, 12, 33–34, 35
    Craftsman dedication to, 21
    Stickley becomes interested in, 17
Russel, Archimedes, 22

S

Safety reminders, 64
Sanding and sandpaper, 78–79
Sap wood, 60
Sargent, Irene, 18–19, 21, 22
    association with Stickley ends, 24
Sawdust, 78
Sawing, 61–62, 64. *See also* Joinery; Routers
Schools and education, 29, 37
Screen,
    from catalog, 59
    project, 93–100
Seat, 45
Seat frame and upholstery, 88
Select lumber, 62
Serving table, 52, 53
Settle,
    from catalog, 44
    project, 129–35
Shaker furniture, 18
Shellac sticks, 78
Shelves. *See* Bookcase
Side chair, 41
Silicon carbide paper, 78
Simmonds Mattress Company, 31
Skaneateles, NY, 32
Sliding head bar clamp, 79
Slivering, 61
Socialism, 12, 14
Society of Craftsmen, 26
Southern pines, 60
Springs (sprung lumber), 63, 64
Staining (finishing), 84, 85, 87
Stains and stained lumber, 63
    glue and, 81
Steam,
    for bending wood, 77–78
    for dents, 78
Stickley, Albert, 17, 18
Stickley, Barbara (daughter). *See* Wiles, Barbara Stickley
Stickley, Barbara (mother), 17
Stickley, Charles, 17, 18
Stickley, Eda Simmons, 17, 24
    death of, 31
Stickley, Gustav, 16, 17–32, 33–38*ff*.
    See also specific projects, techniques
    bankruptcy, later life, 31–32
    death of, 32
    and democratic art, 33–38
    early business life, 17–19
    establishment in Syracuse, 19*ff*.
    European visits, 19, 33

family background, 17
family life with wife, 24
founding of *The Craftsman*, 21–22
move to New York, 24
and New York Craftsman
    Building, 29–31
social and professional associations,
    26
Stickley, J. George, 18, 19, 31
Stickley, Leopold (brother), 19, 31
Stickley, Leopold (father), 17
Stickley Brothers Company, 17–18
Stickley (Gustav) Company, 19–20*ff*.
Stickley (L. & J. G.) Company, 19, 31
Stickley-Simonds Company, 18–19
Stoeckel, Leopold. *See* Stickley,
    Leopold
Stokowski, Leopold, 37
Strap clamp, 79
Sullivan, Louis, 9, 22, 37
Surface finishing, 37, 84–87
Surface preparation, 78–79
Syracuse, NY, 18–24
Syracuse University, 22

T

Tables,
    combination bookcase and table
        (project), 100–6

dining (project), 136–42
from catalog, 46, 47, 48, 49, 52, 53,
    54
router, 75–77
Taboret, 47
Tannic acid, 84
Technology. *See* Machinery
Teflon glides, 82
Tenons. *See* Mortise-and-tenon
    joints; specific projects
Three-fold screen, 59
Tiffany, Louis C., 9, 22
Tile companies and tiles, 15, 19–20

U

United Crafts, The 20*ff*.
    becomes Craftsman Workshops, 25
    ideals and goals of, 21
United Crafts Hall, 22–23
Upholstery, 88

V

Van Briggle Pottery Company, 15
Van Erp, Dirk, 13–14
Veneer, 72–73
Voysee (Arts and Crafts master), 19

W

Warps and warping (warped
    lumber), 61, 63, 64
Water stains, for finishing, 85
Weller, S. A., 14
Who's Who, 26
Wiles, Barbara Stickley (Mrs. Ben),
    31–32
Wood, 37, 60–64. *See also* specific
    projects
    bending, 77–78
    defects in, 63, 64
    determining board feet, 62
    finishing, 37, 84–87
    grading, 62–63
    layout, 64
    ordering, 63
    preparation of, 64
    preparation of surface, 78–79
    Stickley's notes on, 60–62
    veneer, 72–73
Wormholes, filling, 78
Wright, Frank Lloyd, 22
Writing table, 54
Wurlitzer Company, 31

Y

Yates Hotel (Syracuse), 18–19